THE COMPLETE HSA GUIDEBOOK

How to Make Health Savings Accounts Work for You

new

SEVENTH EDITION

Includes health care reform and tax change updates

Stephen D. Neeleman, MD

ISBN: 978-0-9763992-1-6 Printed in the United States of America

FOREWORD

On March 23, 2010, President Obama signed the Patient Protection and Affordable Care Act (PPACA) into law. On June 28, 2012, the Supreme Court of the United States upheld the constitutionality of the major provisions of PPACA. On November 6, 2012, the general population confirmed its acceptance of the law with the convincing general election results in favor of President Obama. After years of debate, PPACA appears to be here to stay.

During the past 10 years, HealthEquity has grown from a simple idea to one of the largest HSA trustees in the United States. We currently provide HSAs for over 24,000 employers. Nearly every day, one of our employers or members asks us if PPACA has hurt HSAs. One common misconception of the new law is that many think the limit for HSA deposits, like FSAs, will decrease to only $2,500 per year. In reality, the amount Americans will be able to deposit tax-free annually into HSAs is based on inflation and will typically increase from year to year. PPACA has no provisions that decrease the amount of money people can put in their HSAs. Thankfully, HSAs are here to stay and they will continue to help people better save and spend their health care dollars.

We began writing the first edition of *The Complete HSA Guidebook* just a few short months after the original HSA law became effective on January 1, 2004. It is remarkable to see the change in people's understanding and acceptance of HSAs over the past 9 years. I recently met with a large and well known technology company that is very excited about offering and educating its employees about the benefits of HSAs. They told me that when they first presented HSAs to their senior management, they were told that HSAs were considered "4-letter words". This company has now embraced HSAs as a key part of their employees' benefits plan and the best way for their people to save tax-free dollars for future health care needs. Best of all, their employees love their HSAs.

While employers save money by offering HSA-qualified health insurance to their employees, perhaps most exciting, is the fact that American tax-payers are using HSAs to increase their personal savings, avoid paying taxes for necessary medical care, and are growing their money, tax-free, for retirement.

HealthEquity was founded in 2002 with a simple mission: "We will save health care by helping people better save and spend their health care dollars". Today, HealthEquity has more than one million members, over 22,000 employer clients, and partners with more than 60 health plans throughout the country to bring HSAs to the market. We are committed to fulfilling our mission to helping people use their HSAs to become healthier and wealthier. As this edition goes to print, HealthEquity members have saved over 1 billion dollars in their HSAs! National HSA balances are estimated to surpass 10 billion dollars.

Our initial goal with *The Complete HSA Guidebook* was to create a book about HSAs that was both comprehensive and easy to understand. I believe we accomplished that goal, as many of our readers have commented on the important role *The Complete HSA Guidebook* has played in helping them better understand HSAs. This sixth edition has been updated to include the most recent regulations from HHS and clarifications from the IRS that affect the HSA law.

I am very appreciative of Sophie Korczyk and Hazel Witte for their work on the first edition. Their legacy is a thoughtful approach to helping our readers understand the complicated tax and insurance laws that affect HSAs. Sadly, Sophie passed away in November 2009.

We remain committed to helping people improve their health and their financial well-being through better understanding and adoption of HSAs. We hope this guidebook remains a powerful tool to accomplish that end.

Stephen D. Neeleman, MD
HealthEquity CEO & Co-Founder
Salt Lake City, Utah
January 2014

TABLE OF CONTENTS

CHAPTER 1

How an HSA Can Benefit You

What Is an HSA?

An HSA is a tax-advantaged savings account that belongs to you. It is always paired with a qualified high-deductible health plan (HDHP).

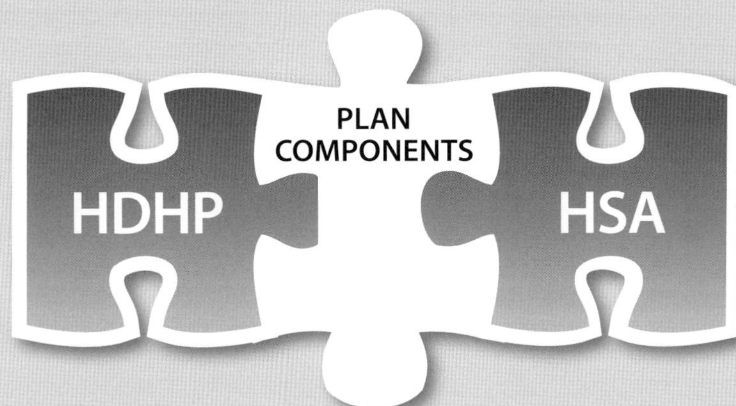

Traditional health plans have higher premiums. At the end of the year, all of the money you have spent on premiums is gone.

Unlike a traditional health plan, a health savings account (HSA)-qualified high-deductible health plan (HDHP), has a lower premium, and some of the money you would have otherwise spent on premiums can go into your HSA instead. Additionally, you save money on taxes and are given more flexibility and control over your health care dollars.

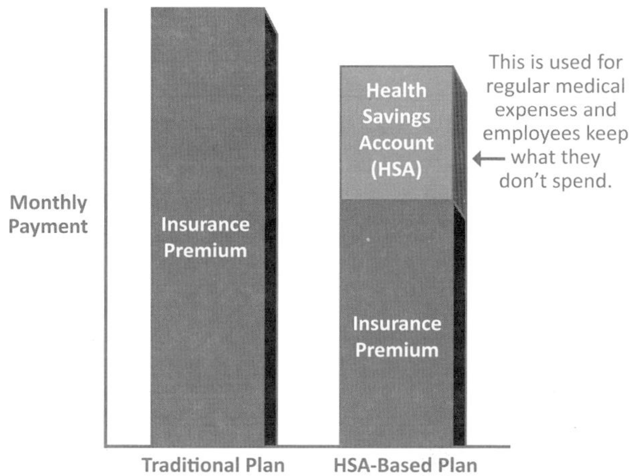

An HSA is administered by a bank, insurance company, or approved third-party custodian or trustee. In most cases, the cash balance is FDIC-insured. Most HSA administrators provide online banking services similar to those of a personal bank account.

You and your employer can make tax-free deposits into your HSA, as long as you are enrolled in a qualified HDHP. The HDHP protects you from major medical costs, such as catastrophic illness, prolonged hospitalization and excessive medical bills.

The HSA covers:

- Your insurance deductible
- Qualified health care expenses that insurance plans might exclude
- Co-payments and coinsurance until you reach your health plan's out-of-pocket maximum (the HDHP covers the rest)

The Money Is Yours

All of the money in the HSA—including any contributions deposited by your employer—remains yours, even if you leave your job, leave your qualifying health plan, or retire.

In other words, an HSA is not a "use-it-or-lose-it" type of account. For this reason, some people use the HSA as an additional savings account for retirement.

You Can Grow Your Account Through Saving or Investing

You decide how to use the HSA money, including whether to save it or spend it for health care expenses.

As your balance rolls over from year to year, it earns interest. When your balance is large enough, you can invest it—tax-free—the same way you can invest dollars from other retirement accounts.

You Gain Triple-Tax Savings

An HSA provides triple-tax savings because:

- Contributions to the HSA are tax-free for you—whether they come from you, your employer, or as gifts from friends or relatives.
- Your account and investment earnings are tax-free.
- You can withdraw your money tax-free at any time, as long as you use it for qualified medical expenses.

You Have More Choice and Flexibility in How You Pay for Health Care

An HSA-qualified HDHP gives you greater choice and flexibility when managing your health care options.

Pay for Qualified Medical Expenses

You can use the HSA to pay for qualified medical expenses for yourself, your spouse, and your dependents before the HDHP deductible is met, as well as for other health care expenses allowed under Section 213(d) of the Internal Revenue Code (IRC). These are generally the same health care expenses individual taxpayers can deduct on their federal income tax returns. The qualified medical expenses are broader than what most health plans cover.

Cover Work/Life Transitions

You can use the HSA to bridge events, such as unemployment, job changes, and periods of disability, by paying for health insurance premiums or health care directly. Your HSA can be used to pay Consolidated Omnibus Budget Reconciliation Act (COBRA) premiums (for continued health care coverage through your former employer), or premiums for long-term care.

Cover Gaps in Care

You can use tax-free HSA dollars for co-payments and deductibles, as well as for services that are not offered by your health plan. You may also pay for services from a physician out of your network with your HSA.

Pay for Post-Retirement Health Care Expenses

HSAs help you save for retirement health expenses tax-free. You can use your HSA to pay for Medicare premiums and out-of-pocket expenses, including deductibles, co-pays, and coinsurance (but not Medigap), including:

- Part A (hospital and inpatient services)
- Part B (physician and outpatient services)
- Part C (Medicare HMO and PPO plans)
- Part D (prescription drugs)

Manage the Variability of Expenses

The HSA also allows you to deal with the variability of health care expenses. For example, one year you may have just a few medical appointments, whereas the next year you may meet the deductible mid-year and still have more appointments.

Because the HSA allows you to reimburse yourself at any time, you can choose to save your money for times when you have more expenses.

With combined HSA funds from the previous year, in addition to the funds added during the current year, you may be able to meet all of your costs tax-free.

Benefit from a Healthy Lifestyle

Beginning in 2011, all new HSA-qualified health plans are required to cover 100% of standard preventive care services, and have a fixed limit on your out-of-pocket costs.

If you take advantage of preventive care services and adopt healthy lifestyle habits, your HSA can grow tax-free from year to year and become a significant addition to your retirement nest egg.

Help Manage Costs

With an HSA-qualified health plan, you have significant power and responsibility over your health care decisions. Policymakers hope that by having such a financial incentive, participants become influential health care consumers who demand and receive better value with their health care spending.

How Do HSAs Compare to IRAs or 401(k) Plans?

HSAs have features in common with retirement accounts, such as individual retirement accounts (IRAs) and 401(k) plans that keep their tax advantages when used for specific purposes. These advantages include year-to-year rollover, portability, choice of account investments, and survivor benefits.

Variations on that approach, including Roth IRAs, 529 education accounts, and Coverdell accounts, have helped consumers grow their retirement nest eggs using tax-free savings accounts.

How an HSA Is Like a 401(k) or an IRA

- You and your employer can make pre-tax contributions to your HSA.
- Your contributions roll over from year to year.
- Your HSA can grow tax-free for as long as you own the account.
- Your HSA can be inherited by your survivors.

How an HSA Is Better

- You and your employer do not need to pay FICA (Social Security) tax on your HSA contributions made through payroll.

- You can keep your money liquid in an FDIC-insured bank account or, when the balance grows large enough, you can invest it.

- You can contribute money from both earned and unearned income up to the IRS yearly limit, as long as you are covered by an HSA-qualified HDHP and are not enrolled in Medicare. Family members and other individuals can contribute to your account, however, only you and your employer may take tax deductions.

- You can use the money for the health care expenses of your spouse and any of your IRS-qualified dependents—tax-free.

- If you are no longer employed, you can still make contributions to your HSA as long as you're still covered by an HSA-qualified HDHP and are not enrolled in Medicare.

- As long as you use the funds for qualified medical expenses, you are not required to be of retirement age to make tax-free withdrawals at any time without tax or penalty.

- After age 65, you can spend the HSA money on non-medical items without paying a 20% penalty. However, you will have to pay income tax on distributions if they are not used for qualified medical expenses.

Who Can Establish and Contribute to an HSA?

The IRS has strict guidelines to determine who is eligible to own and contribute to an HSA.

Definition of an Eligible Individual

Under the law, an eligible individual:

- Must be covered under a qualified HDHP on the first day of any month for which eligibility is claimed.
- May not be covered under any health plan that is not a qualified HDHP, with the exception of certain permitted coverage and certain health-related payment plans discussed in Chapter 2.
- Must not be enrolled in Medicare (the health care component of the Social Security program).
- May not be claimed as a dependent on another individual's tax return.

Health Care Reform and Adult Children Covered by Your HDHP

Under the Patient Protection and Affordable Care Act (PPACA), adult children up to the age of 26 can be covered by their parent's HDHP and use funds from the parent's HSA. However, if the adult child is self-supporting or does not qualify as a tax deduction, that child cannot use funds from the parent's HSA.

Single adult children who have coverage under a parent's family HDHP can open their own HSAs and contribute up to the yearly family maximum—$6,550 for 2014. While spouses must split the family maximum contribution; adult children can each contribute the entire family maximum to their own HSAs.

This is an excellent opportunity to set your adult child up with his or her own HSA as a tax-free gift (you do not get to deduct the contribution, but your child can receive it tax-free).

Employed Individuals

An employer may offer an HDHP with an HSA and pay for some or all of the HDHP premium and contribute an allotted amount toward an HSA. The employer may also offer an HDHP only and allow a certain amount for other benefits, including an HSA, perhaps through a cafeteria plan. In either of these cases, the participant is the eligible individual and owner of the HSA. Therefore, the law's requirements have been met.

Employers may have additional requirements for employees who want to participate in a health plan, including those with an eligible HDHP, who want to contribute to an HSA.

These eligibility requirements are separate from those required by law and are part of many employer-sponsored health plans. It is important that employees understand all eligibility requirements in order to reduce misunderstanding or confusion that can occur when a new type of health plan is implemented.

Health plans typically require new employees to work for the employer for a short period of time before becoming eligible to participate. Unless the employee is covered by some other qualifying HDHP during this period, he or she may have to suspend HSA contributions until resuming coverage under a qualified HDHP.

Self-Employed and Unemployed Individuals

If an individual is a subchapter S owner, self-employed, or unemployed, the individual can open an HSA and make contributions as long as all IRS eligibility requirements are met.

Retired and Disabled Individuals

If an otherwise eligible person is not enrolled in Medicare, even though that individual has reached age 65, he or she can contribute to an HSA until the month they are enrolled in Medicare. The individual may also continue to make catch-up contributions prior to their enrollment in Medicare.

You are not eligible to set up an HSA if you do not have an HDHP. Medicare is considered first-dollar coverage, not an HDHP. If you are enrolled in Medicare, you are ineligible to set up or contribute to an HSA.

Age Is Not the Issue

Regardless of your age, you may still set up and contribute to an HSA as long as you have a qualified HDHP and are not enrolled in Medicare.

If you have an HDHP as well as access to a "retirement" health reimbursement arrangement (HRA) that provides reimbursement only after you retire, you may still set up an HSA.

Disability Benefits and HSAs

If you are covered by an HDHP/HSA and qualify for short-term or long-term disability benefits under an employer-sponsored plan, nothing should change if the basic health care coverage arrangement remains intact during the disability period.

If you decide to apply for Social Security Disability Insurance (SSDI) benefits, everything changes because you cease to be an eligible individual.

Determining If an HSA Is Right for You

An HSA allows you to be more involved with decisions on how your health care dollars are actually spent and encourages you to budget effectively and save money. In order to think in terms of a health care budget, you want to look at your financial situation and the type of health care you require.

Consider whether you are able to establish and contribute to an HSA, have benefits paid from one, or claim the tax deduction for a contribution. Whether an HDHP/HSA is right for you depends on a number of factors, including the health needs of you and your family, in addition to the frequency you may expect to change jobs and/or health plans.

Do You Want to Build a Fund for Health Care Expenses After Retirement?

Even with the passage of PPACA and changes in Medicare, post-retirement health care costs are expected to escalate rapidly. Industry analysts warn that many retirees will fall short of the amounts needed to cover the gaps in medical coverage as they age.

Without an HSA, many retirees are now paying for the non-covered portion of their medical expenses by taking distributions from their 401(k)s and other retirement savings plans. Unfortunatley, these individuals must pay income tax on those distributions.

With an HSA, a retiree can save significant amounts of money on taxes by paying for qualified medical expenses with pretax dollars.

Do You Use Substantial Amounts of Health Care?

Any time you have a choice of health plans, whether from a selection of plans offered by your employer, or as an individual purchaser, consider the patterns in your health care use.

A chronic condition is one that lasts a long time, or recurs frequently, and can be treated but not cured. Some people with chronic conditions may need substantial health care on an ongoing basis. An HSA may be beneficial for you or a family member who suffers from a chronic disease, such as diabetes, heart dysfunction, or asthma. Some HDHP policies pay for medications associated with chronic condition first dollar (not subject to your deductible) under preventative care coverage.

Not all chronic conditions are exceedingly cost-intensive. However, they may need monitoring. Some require medical appliances that are not typically provided by health plans, but are considered medical expenses for purposes of an HSA. Therefore, the expenditure is payable from an HSA account.

Before committing to an HSA plan, you will want to compare the flexibility and tax advantages of HSA distributions with the coverage offered by low-deductible health plans to determine which option is right for you.

With increasing co-payments and coinsurance in traditional plans, you will find that HSAs are often the right choice.

Do You Need Health Care Coverage for that Unanticipated Expense or Disaster?

Although you and your family may be in good health, health care coverage is necessary in the event that a damaging and unanticipated accident may occur.

Acknowledge whether or not you can set aside money in an HSA on a regular basis to cover your annual bout with the flu or your child's ear infection.

Many people do not reach their deductibles, because they do not spend much on health care. An HSA-qualified health plan may be just right for you. It gives you control over your spending and allows you to save tax-free in an account you can use if and when your health care spending increases.

Are You Willing to Use Your Plan's Network?

HDHPs typically offer networks of providers that have agreed to give special pricing to participants in plans they have contracts with. Discounts lower the amount you may need to pay out of your HSA.

Are you willing to use doctors in your plan's network to lower your health care costs? If you decide to go out-of-network, are you willing to pay for the higher costs, possibly out of your HSA or pocket?

The HSA gives you flexibility to go to an out-of-network doctor. If the money is in your HSA, you can pay for that visit.

The HSA-qualified health plan is based on making good choices, both health-wise and budget-wise.

Do You Change Jobs Often?

Consider your job, your industry, or occupation and your career stage and career plans.

People tend to change jobs more often in some fields than in others and younger people tend to move around more than people more established in their careers.

HDHPs can be extended under COBRA like any other plan, and you can use your HSA to pay COBRA premiums during a period when you lack other coverage.

You can continue to use your HSA for health care expenses even if you do not have other coverage. An HSA can be an important safety net in a difficult economy.

CHAPTER 2

HSA-Compatible Health Plans

The Qualified High-Deductible Health Plan (HDHP)

Before you open an HSA, the IRS requires that you enroll in a qualified high-deductible health plan (HDHP). The HDHP is the insurance component of HSA-based health coverage.

What are the Components of a HDHP?

An HDHP has:

- A lower monthly premium than typical health plans
- A higher annual deductible than typical health plans
- A maximum limit on the total amount you are required to pay out of your own pocket for the deductible, covered medical expenses, co-payments, and coinsurance (premiums are not included in this maximum limit)

Plans that satisfy certain deductible and out-of-pocket limits are referred to as HSA-qualified HDHPs.

The following table shows the minimum annual deductible that a health plan must have, in order to qualify as an HDHP. Conversely, it also shows the maximum annual deductible and other out-of-pocket expenses for HDHPs for 2013.

	Self-Only Coverage	Family Coverage
Minimum annual deductible	$1,250	$2,500
Maximum annual deductible and other out-of-pocket expenses*	$6,350	$12,700

* This limit does not apply to deductibles and expenses for out-of-network services if the plan uses a network of providers. Instead, only deductibles and out-of-pocket expenses for services within the network are used to figure whether the limit applies.

** If a plan requires an individual to spend more than this amount on the deductible and other out-of-pocket expenses for in-network covered medical expenses, it is not an HSA-qualified HDHP.

Self-Only HDHP Coverage

Self-only HDHP coverage is an HDHP that covers only one eligible individual.

Family HDHP Coverage

Family HDHP coverage is an HDHP that covers an eligible individual and at least one other individual, even if the additional individual is not HSA eligible (for example, if the other individual has a self only plan that does not allow them to contribute to an HSA).

Example

Family Coverage

Bill and Sue are married. Bill selects coverage from his employer that covers both him and Sue. Sue has her own self-only policy from her employer that is not HDHP qualified.

Bill can make a full family contribution to an HSA, provided he has no other disqualifying coverage.

Employee Plus One HDHP

If an eligible individual and his or her dependent child are covered under an employee plus one HDHP offered by the individual's employer, the IRS considers them to have family HDHP coverage.

Family Plans That Do Not Meet the High-Deductible Rule

Some family plans have deductibles for both the entire family and individual family members. If you meet the individual deductible for one family member under these plans, you are not required to meet the higher annual deductible for the family.

If either the deductible for the entire family or the deductible for an individual family member is less than the minimum annual deductible for family coverage allowed by the IRS, the plan is not considered an HSA-qualified HDHP.

Example

HDHP with Both an Individual Deductible and a Family Deductible

Elliott has family health insurance coverage for 2014, with an annual deductible of $3,500 and an individual deductible of $1,500 for each family member.

The plan does not qualify as an HSA-qualified HDHP, because the deductible for an individual family member is below the minimum annual deductible of $2,500 for family coverage in 2014.

What Does an HDHP Cover?

The purpose of the HDHP is to cover higher, unexpected health care expenses that would be difficult to pay for out-of-pocket, even with an HSA.

Under PPACA, HDHPs are also required to pay for preventative care services.

Exactly what your plan covers depends on your employer, your insurer, and the choices you make from among the plans available to you. For example, some plans may pay for fertility treatments or bariatric (weight loss) surgery, while others may not.

There are variations among HDHPs, so do not assume that your next plan covers the same things as your last. Be sure you understand your new plan's provisions, found in the summary of benefits you receive during enrollment.

Important Insurance Terms

There are some terms that will be essential to your understanding of various types of HDHP's, as well as your ability to compare their features.

Eligible Individual

You qualify as an eligible individual if you meet the IRS eligibility requirements for opening and contributing to an HSA:

- You must be covered under an HSA-qualified HDHP on the first day of the month in which you open an HSA or make a contribution to an HSA.
- You have no other health coverage, unless permitted under IRS guidelines (see "Insurance Coverage Permitted with an HSA" later in this chapter).
- You are not enrolled in Medicare.
- You cannot be claimed as a dependent on someone else's tax return.

Although you must be an eligible individual to open or contribute to an HSA, you do not have to be covered under an HDHP to keep the account, earn tax-free interest and investment dividends, or make tax-free distributions for eligible medical expenses. You get to keep, grow, and spend all of the money in the account long after you leave your employer or HDHP.

Full-Contribution or Last-Month Rule

The full-contribution rule (also known as the last-month rule) allows individuals who are eligible on the first day of the last month of their tax-paying year (December 1 for most tax-payers) to be considered eligible for the entire year. Therefore, under these circumstances, you can contribute up to the full yearly maximum for your coverage type (self or family).

In this case, an eligible individual is considered enrolled in the same HDHP coverage (i.e., self-only or family coverage) as he or she has previously been on the first day of the last month of the year. For example, if an individual first becomes HSA-eligible on Dec. 1, 2014, and has family HDHP coverage, he or she is considered an eligible individual having family HDHP coverage for all 12 months in 2014.

The full contribution rule also applies to catch-up contributions made by eligible individuals age 55 and older, who are allowed to contribute an additional $1,000 each year.

The full-contribution rule applies regardless of whether the individual was eligible for the entire year, had HDHP coverage for the entire year, or had disqualifying non-HDHP coverage for part of the year. However, a testing period applies for purposes of the full-contribution rule. If you fail to maintain an HSA-qualified HDHP during the entire testing period, you will have to pay taxes and penalties for making an excess contribution (see more about the testing period in the next section).

Examples

Using the Full-Contribution Rule To Make the Largest Allowable HSA Contribution

Roberto's HDHP coverage started on Nov. 10, 2013. Because he has HDHP coverage by December 1, he can contribute $3,250 to his HSA as if he had been in the HDHP the entire year.

Karl joined his HDHP on Nov. 30, 2013. He waits until February 2014 to open his HSA. The IRS allows account holders to make 2013 contributions until April 15, 2014, so Karl makes a lump sum contribution of $3,250 for 2013. He also starts contributing for 2014 by setting up regular payroll deductions.

Nancy joined her HDHP on Dec. 2, 2013. She cannot make a full-year contribution for 2013 like Roberto and Karl did, because she missed the December 1 deadline for being in a qualified HDHP. In fact, she cannot contribute for the month of December, because she has to be in an HDHP on the first day of the month in which she makes a contribution to her HSA. The first day she is eligible to contribute to her HSA is Jan. 1, 2014.

Testing Period

Under the full-contribution rule, the testing period begins with the last month of your tax year and ends on the last day of the twelfth month following that month. For example, December 1, 2013, through December 31, 2014.

If contributions were made to your HSA based on your eligibility for the entire year under the full-contribution rule, you must remain an eligible individual during the testing period.

If you fail to remain an eligible individual during the testing period (with the exception of death or disability), you must include the total number of contributions made to your HSA that would not have otherwise been made, apart from the full-contribution rule as income.

This amount must be included in your income, in the year that you fail to be an eligible individual. This amount is also subject to an additional 10% tax. Income and additional tax are shown on IRS Form 8889, Part III.

Example

Not Remaining an Eligible Individual for the Entire Testing Period

Chris, 53, becomes an eligible individual on December 1, 2013. He has family HDHP coverage on that date. Under the last-month rule, he can contribute $6,450 to his HSA for 2013.

Chris stops being an eligible individual in June 2014, because he drops his HDHP coverage. Because Chris did not remain an eligible individual during the testing period (December 1, 2013, through December 31, 2014), the contributions made in 2014 that would not have been made without the full-contribution rule must be included in his 2014 income.

Chris uses the worksheet for line 3 of IRS Form 8889 instructions to determine this amount.

January	0
February	0
March	0
April	0
May	0
June	0
July	0
August	0
September	0
October	0
November	0
December	$6,450
Total for All Months	$6,450

Divide Total by 12 for Monthly Contribution $537.50.

Chris would include $5,912.50 ($6,450 minus the $537.50 that was allowable for the one month he was eligible in 2013) in his gross income on his 2014 tax return. Also, an additional 10% tax applies to the $5,912.50 he over-contributed in 2013.

Example

Changing to Family Coverage

Erika, 39, has self-only HDHP coverage on January 1, 2014. After the birth of her baby, she gets family HDHP coverage on November 1, 2014. Because Erika has family HDHP coverage on Dec. 1, 2014, she contributes $6,550 for the last two months of 2014.

Erika uses the worksheet for line 3 of IRS Form 8889 instructions to calculate the amounts she contributed for the months she had single coverage, and the amounts she contributed for the months she had family coverage.

Shown below is how Erika calculates the allowable maximum HSA contribution for a year when she has two kinds of coverage (single and family):

Months	Coverage Type	Monthly Prorated Contribution
January – October	Single	$3,300 / 12 = $275.00 per month
In November, Erika became eligible to make the larger HSA contribution for a family.		
November – December	Family	$6,550 / 12 = $545.83 per month
Add the prorated allowable contribution for each month		$3,841.67

Deductible

A deductible is the amount of covered expenses that an individual must pay for a given plan year before the insurance company starts paying covered medical claims. Claims for preventive care are usually paid by the insurance company without requiring you to apply your deductible (see the section on "First-Dollar Coverage for Preventive Care" later in this chapter).

The plan year may be the calendar year (January 1 to December 31), or some other 12-month period that your employer or insurer chooses for managing your plan and keeping track of deductibles and other limits (some plans allow deductibles to accumulate for more than 12 months—see "Carry-Over Deductibles" in this section).

To qualify for an HSA in 2013 and 2014, a single person must have an HDHP with a deductible of at least $1,250. The minimum allowable deductible for a family is $2,500.

The HDHP must also have a limit on the maximum deductible and maximum out-of-pocket amounts (it is possible for an HDHP to have a deductible that is too high to qualify for use with an HSA).

The deductible and out-of-pocket limits are subject to change annually due to increases in the consumer price index (CPI). The IRS typically announces changes to these limits in June, the year before they change.

Tax Year 2014		
	Self-Only Coverage	Family Coverage
Minimum annual deductible	$1,250	$2,500
Maximum annual deductible and other out-of-pocket expenses*	$6,350	$12,700

* This limit does not apply to deductibles and expenses for out-of-network services if the plan uses a network of providers. Instead, only deductibles and out-of-pocket expenses for services within the network should be used to figure whether the limit applies.

** If a plan requires an individual to spend more than this amount on the deductible and other out-of-pocket expenses for covered medical expenses, it is not an HSA-qualified HDHP.

Not all HDHPs meet IRS requirements. A plan with a deductible that is too high will be disqualified for use with an HSA.

Embedded Deductibles

Some HDHPs provide multiple deductibles or embedded deductibles. In such plans, the lowest deductible is the one that determines whether the plan is a qualified HDHP.

Example

Family Plan with Embedded Deductibles that Disqualify the Plan as an HDHP

The Jones family is covered under a plan that provides family coverage with a per-person embedded deductible of $1,000 and a total family deductible of $2,500 (also called an umbrella deductible).

The plan begins paying for care for individuals in the family who exceed $1,000 in expenses, regardless of whether the total $2,500 family deductible has been met.

Mr. Jones incurs covered medical expenses of $1,500 during the year.

The plan pays benefits of $500 on his behalf, even though the $2,500 family deductible has not been met.

Since claims are paid by the insurance company for individuals before they reach the $2,500 minimum family deductible, the plan is not a qualified HDHP, and the family therefore is not eligible to contribute to an HSA.

Without the $1,000 per-person deductible, however, the plan would be an eligible HDHP.

Carry-Over Deductible

Some insurance carriers allow expenses that were applied to the previous deductible to be applied to, or carried over, to the new policy when the plan year resets. Usually, the carry-over deductible is applied for expenses incurred at the end of the plan year during a certain period of time (usually one to three months before the plan year's end).

This is not a requirement, but it is an added benefit when expenses occur late in the year. Only in rare circumstances will this type of carry-over deductible exclude your plan from being HSA-qualified. Because the deductible includes more than 12 months, the IRS minimum deductible limit (based on a 12-month plan year) must be increased.

Example

Carry-Over Deductible

Matt has a plan that allows him to include expenses from 15 months (three month carry-over) to satisfy the deductible.

To be an HSA-qualified HDHP, an individual policy must have a minimum deductible in 2014 of $1,562.50 (15/12 x $1,250 = $1,562.50). A family policy must have a minimum deductible of $3,125 (15/12 x $2,500 = $3,125).

If Matt's plan does not satisfy these increased minimums, it is not considered a qualified HDHP.

First-Dollar Coverage for Preventive Care

First-dollar coverage is coverage that pays the entire eligible amount, without requiring that you meet your deductible.

Beginning September 23, 2010, PPACA required all new group health plans and plans in the individual market to provide first-dollar coverage for preventive services rated A or B by the U.S. Preventive Services Task Force. These include recommended immunizations, preventive care for infants, children, and adolescents, as well as additional preventive care and screenings for women.

Existing (grandfathered) HDHPs may continue to provide coverage for preventive care without a deductible, or with a deductible below the minimum annual deductible.

Preventive care includes, but is not limited to the following:

- Periodic health evaluations, including tests and diagnostic procedures ordered in connection with routine examinations, such as annual physicals
- Routine prenatal and well-child care
- Child and adult immunizations
- Tobacco cessation programs
- Obesity weight-loss programs
- Screening services, including screening services for the following:
    - Cancer
    - Heart and vascular diseases
    - Infectious diseases
    - Mental health conditions
    - Substance abuse
    - Metabolic, nutritional, and endocrine conditions
    - Musculoskeletal disorders
    - Obstetric and gynecological conditions
    - Pediatric conditions
    - Vision and hearing disorders

Important Details

- The first-dollar coverage required by PPACA applies to people enrolled in job-related health plans or individual health insurance policies created after March 23, 2010. If you are in such a health plan, this provision will affect you as soon as your plan begins its first new plan year on or after September 23, 2010.

- If your health plan uses a network of providers, be aware that health plans are only required to provide these preventive services through an in-network provider. Your health plan may allow you to receive these services from an out-of-network provider, but may charge you an additional fee.

To know which covered preventive services are right for you—based on your age, gender, and health status, ask your health care provider.

IRS Rules for Preventive Care Benefits

Even with the passage of health care reform, IRS rules for first-dollar coverage remain in place. The IRS states that benefits eligible for first-dollar coverage can include:

- Periodic health evaluations, including tests and diagnostic procedures ordered in connection with routine examinations, such as annual physicals
- Routine prenatal and well-child care
- Child and adult immunizations
- Tobacco cessation programs
- Obesity weight-loss programs
- Screening services
- Some medications which are intended to prevent disease (such as high blood pressure or high cholesterol medications)

The definition of preventive care that applies to HSA-qualified HDHPs generally excludes any service or benefit intended to treat an existing illness, injury, or condition. However, in situations where it would be unreasonable to perform another procedure to treat the condition, incidental treatments, or ancillary to a preventive care screening or service is allowed.

If you have questions about whether the new health care reform provisions apply to your particular plan, contact your insurer or plan administrator. If you still have questions, contact your state insurance department.

State Law and Preventive Care

PPACA allows states to adopt and enforce laws and regulations that afford greater consumer protections while ensuring a basic level of security across the country. If a state adopts or has a pre-existing requirement that meets the federal standards, then it retains the authority to enforce it. Therefore, under PPACA, states are allowed to require insurers to offer first-dollar preventive care services beyond the minimum services required by the federal government.

The HSA law uses a federal definition of preventive care. Therefore, individuals and some employers in states whose laws require first-dollar coverage for benefits that do not fit the federal definition may be unable to participate in HSA-qualified HDHPs. In such states, only those employers who offer self-insured plans will be able to adopt HSAs/HDHPs (self-insured plans are those under which the employer pays for medical claims as they arise, rather than contracting for coverage from an insurer).

Several states are in the process of changing state law to allow for HSAs by exempting HDHP/HSA plans from state benefit mandates.

Network Plans

A network plan (such as a PPO) is a health plan that generally accommodates favorable pricing and benefits for services provided by its network of providers, as opposed to services provided outside of the network.

Repricing

If your HDHP is a network plan, your expenses will be repriced if you use in-network health care providers. Repricing refers to the adjustment of health care providers' prices, to reflect discounts the providers have negotiated with your health plan.

Network plans and repricing are both allowable, but are not required in qualified HDHPs.

Separate Out-of-Pocket Limits

Network plans may provide a different level of benefits for members when they use in-network versus out-of-network providers. Many of these plans have separate out-of-pocket limits and deductibles for network and non-network care. This provides a powerful incentive for plan participants to use network providers.

The law does not specify a maximum out-of-pocket limit for spending on non-network care, so an HDHP may have higher out-of-pocket limits for services provided outside the network than the $6,350/$12,700 limits for 2014.

Usual, Customary, and Reasonable Amounts

A plan may also restrict benefits to what is considered usual, customary, and reasonable amounts. Any expenses above that amount that are not paid by an HDHP are not required to be included in determining maximum out-of-pocket expenses.

Example

Fee Charged by an Out-of-Network Provider

Your plan determines that the reasonable cost of a certain type of surgery is $2,000, a price it has negotiated with its in-network providers. You go to an out-of-network provider and the bill totals $2,500. The health plan can pay only $2,000 of this bill, and the additional $500 you have to pay may not apply to your health plan's out-of-pocket limit.

Inquire as to whether your HDHP has separate limits for in- and out-of-network providers and whether its network includes the providers you want to use for medical care. You may obtain this information by speaking with your employer's benefits administrator, your insurance plan, your HR team, or by reading the summary of plan benefits available from your plan or given to you during open enrollment.

Co-Payments and Coinsurance

A co-payment is a fixed-dollar payment the patient makes per doctor visit, treatment, study, or prescription.

Coinsurance is the percentage of an insurance claim for which the patient is responsible.

Pre-Existing Conditions

Getting a Certificate of Continuous Coverage

PPACA requires that eligible, uninsured individuals have access to coverage that does not impose any coverage exclusions for pre-existing health conditions. This provision became effective in 2010 with the establishment of temporary high risk pools. These high risk pools will be superceded by health care exchanges in 2014, which will also offer coverage to people with pre-existing conditions.

However, as Health and Human Services clarifies health care reform provisions by issuing supplemental regulations, disputes and disagreements arise between them and some insurance carriers. It will take time to address all of the questions surrounding pre-existing conditions. In the meantime, there are two approaches available to you:

- If you are applying for an HDHP without employer sponsorship, you might not be covered for pre-existing conditions. However, you can still pay for health expenses for such conditions out of your HSA.
- If you have had continuous health insurance coverage, any conditions considered pre-existing may be covered by your new HDHP sooner than any required wait time, if you have a certificate of coverage from your last insurer as proof of your continuous health insurance coverage.

A written certificate issued by a group health plan or health insurance issuer shows your prior health coverage (creditable coverage). A certificate must be issued automatically and free of charge when you lose coverage under a plan, are entitled to elect COBRA continuation coverage, or when you lose COBRA continuation coverage.

You may need to provide this certificate to your new plan if medical advice, diagnosis, care, or treatment was recommended or received for the condition within six-months prior to your enrollment in the new plan. Some carriers may require as much as an 18-month look-back period.

If you become covered under another group health plan, check with the plan administrator to see if you need to provide this certificate. You may also need this certificate to buy an insurance plan for you or your family, so that it does not exclude coverage for medical conditions that are present before you enroll in the HDHP.

Out-of-Pocket Maximum

The out-of-pocket maximum is the highest amount of money you have to pay during a plan year. In many HDHPs, the out-of-pocket maximum and the deductible are the same amount.

However, many plans do not completely cover expenses once you have reached the deductible. In the following scenario, a plan may "split the bill" with a member until the out-of pocket maximum is reached. This is called coinsurance.

Example

Out-of-Pocket Maximum

Tricia has a deductible of $1,500 and an out-of-pocket maximum of $3,000.

Tricia pays up to her $1,500 deductible, after which her plan agrees to split the bill 80/20. The plan will pay 80% of costs after the deductible, and Tricia will pay 20% in coinsurance .

If Tricia has another $9,500 in expenses after she reaches her deductible, she will pay 20% of that bill until she spends another $1,500 in out-of-pocket expenses.

At this point, her total spending will have reached $3,000. She has hit her out-of-pocket maximum, and her insurance plan will pay 100% of the rest of her covered medical expenses for that plan year.

The amounts you pay for deductibles, co-payments, or coinsurance are included in your out-of-pocket expenses, which are kept as a running total.

Insurance premiums you pay are not included toward out-of-pocket limits.

Once you have reached your plan's limit for the year, remaining eligible expenses are covered100%, regardless of the plan's usual co-payment or coinsurance arrangements. Some plans refer to this limit as the stop-loss limit.

In 2014 , a qualified HDHP's out-of-pocket limits must be no higher than $6,350 per year for individual coverage and no higher than $12,700 per year for family coverage, though they can be lower.

If a plan has multiple out-of-pocket maximums, the sum of these limits must be equal to, or less than the amount required by law.

Remember, the maximum out-of-pocket expenses allowed by law are for in-network care only. Health plans will most likely require higher out-of-pocket expenses for out-of-network care.

Example

Multiple Out-of-Pocket Maximum Limits for a Family

Dean, Laurie, and their two children have a family plan. Their plan specifies that each family member's in-network out-of-pocket maximum is $2,500, after which the plan pays 100% for each member that reaches that maximum.

Since the out-of-pocket maximum per family member by law is $12,700 for 2014, their plan would be a qualified HDHP (4 x $2,500 = $10,000).

However, if they had four children, their plan would not be a qualified HDHP, because the maximum out-of-pocket limit would be higher than the legal maximum (6 x $2,500 = $15,000).

Yearly and Lifetime Limits

Before health care reform, if you exceeded your plan's yearly or lifetime benefit limits for a medical condition, you had to use your HSA or other funds to make up the difference.

PPACA now prohibits insurers from imposing lifetime limits on benefits. This provision became effective September 23, 2010 and affects all existing insurance plans.

If you have been using your HSA or other funds to pay for treatments that exceeded your plan's annual limits, you may be able to stop and have the plan pick up the cost again. Contact your insurance company to find out when it will put this option into effect.

Insurance Coverage Permitted with an HSA

The IRS is very strict about what kinds of insurance you can have along with an HSA-qualified HDHP. Having another policy with benefits that overlap some of the medical coverage in your HDHP can make you ineligible to contribute to an HSA.

The listed benefits outlined below are among some of the insurance policies that can result in ineligibility.

Prescription Drug Benefits

Some plans offer prescription drug benefits through separate plans (also called pharmacy riders), that cover prescription drugs outside of any deductibles that apply to other services covered under the plan. Such prescription drug benefits are not considered permitted coverage under HSA law, unless these riders are specifically designed for preventive care medications.

A participant covered by an HDHP that meets the law's requirements and is also covered by a non-preventive prescription drug plan or rider that provides benefits before the HDHP's deductible is met, may not open or contribute to an HSA. This is because the prescription plan provides first-dollar coverage for a benefit that is not permitted.

Discount Cards

Discount cards that entitle you to price reductions on services or health products, such as prescription drugs, are allowed with the HSA as long as you are required to pay the cost of the items (at the reduced rate), until your deductible is met.

Hospitalization Indemnity Plans

In order to qualify for benefits under Hospitalization Indemnity Plans, you must be admitted to a hospital.

An indemnity plan is one that pays health insurance benefits in the form of cash payments rather than services, typically as a fixed cash amount each day you are in the hospital. Some insurance vendors may call these plans gap plans or HSA protector policies, because one function of such plans is to cover you against a large bill before you meet your HDHPs deductible.

This can serve to protect your HSA dollars, or to help pay for hospital expenses before you have had time to build your account balance.

HSA-qualified indemnity or gap plans cannot cover outpatient hospital services, such as medical tests you might have in a hospital or hospital-related facility without being admitted to the hospital. In other words, the indemnity plan is not intended to cover relatively small expenses just because they are incurred in the hospital rather than in a freestanding facility.

Other Permitted and Non-Permitted Coverage

The IRS has specific rules for insurance plans that are allowed to coexist with an HSA and plans that would disqualify you from owning an HSA. For a quick summary, see the following table:

Allowed	
• Automobile, dental, vision, disability, and long-term care insurance • Coverage for a specific disease or illness as long as it pays a specific dollar amount when the policy is triggered; or indemnity plans that pay a fixed amount per day or other period of hospitalization • Wellness programs offered by employers, if they do not pay significant medical benefits • FSAs or HRAs that are limited purpose (limited to dental, vision, or preventive care) or post-deductible (pay for medical expenses after the plan deductible is met)	• An employer-sponsored HRA that can only be used when you retire or after you meet your annual deductible. • A high-deductible, non-HDHP (PPO, HMO), if the deductible meets or exceeds the HDHP required minimum • An embedded individual deductible in your family HDHP coverage, if it is not less than the minimum required family HDHP deductible • Worker's compensation insurance • Tort liability payments • Prescription or other discount programs that are not insurance

Not Allowed	
• Spouse's flexible spending account (FSA) or health reimbursement arrangement (HRA), if it can pay for any kind of qualified medical expense before the HDHP deductible is met • Health benefits or prescription drugs received from the Veterans Administration or one of its facilities in the last three months • Medicare	• Employer payments or reimbursements for medical expenses below the minimum HDHP deductible • General FSAs or HRAs that pay for any kind of qualified medical expense before the HDHP deductible is met • TRICARE • Social Security Disability Insurance (SSDI)

CHAPTER 3

How to Open an HSA

To open an HSA, you must be enrolled in a qualified HDHP and be otherwise eligible as of the first of the month you want to open your account.

See Chapter 2 for a description of an HSA-qualified HDHP. Your insurance provider, broker or employer can also help you find the right plan.

Find the Right HSA Provider

Not All HSAs Are the Same

You cannot simply set aside your HSA contributions in a shoebox, safe-deposit box, or ordinary bank or other account—the money has to be set aside in an account specifically designated as an HSA.

What a Custodian Does

The HSA trustee or custodian holds your balances, receives and records contributions, and processes distributions. The custodian also prepares the appropriate tax forms for you at the end of the year.

In general, an insurance company or a bank can be an HSA trustee or custodian, as can any entity approved by the Internal Revenue Service (IRS) as a trustee or custodian for individual retirement accounts (IRAs).

Other entities may request approval to be an HSA trustee or custodian under IRS regulations.

Be warned! Not all of these companies provide the same level of service or support. Do your homework about the quality of product and service offered before you sign up with an HSA custodian.

Choosing an HSA Custodian

You may be setting up an HSA on your own, or your employer may make arrangements for you to establish an HSA with a particular HSA administrator.

Your HDHP and HSA do not have to be managed by the same company; you may prefer the service, terms, and investment opportunities of an HSA provider independent from your insurance company.

It is important that your expectations for the basic administration of your HSA are clear. Some of the issues you should examine include fees, investment earnings, and how your account will be managed.

Get Answers to the Following Questions, So Your HSA Runs Smoothly

- **How much should I contribute and how often?**
- **Can I make a contribution monthly, quarterly, or with any payroll?**
- **What methods can I use to make contributions?**
- **How often do I receive a statement?**
- **How often can I increase or decrease my contribution?**
- **When will I receive my debit card and other welcome materials?**
- **What should I do if I need to use the acount before I get my debit card?**

Ask the Following Questions About Fees

- **How are fees set?**
  It costs money to manage your account, keep records, and send out the appropriate forms and statements.

- **Is the fee based on the amount in my account or on how much I contribute monthly? Or is it a fixed fee that is independent of how much I have in my HSA? Are fees waived if my balance reaches a certain level?**

- **Which fees can be assessed?**
  Some possible fees include those for account maintenance, replacement of lost or stolen checks, stop-payment charges if you should have a dispute with a health care provider, or if an erroneous charge to your account is made.

- **Will I be charged a fee if the account is rolled over to another custodian or permanently closed?**
  The disclosure rules apply to account fees and depend on the custodian selected. Fee disclosure rules are different for banks, insurance companies, mutual funds, and other entities.

- **If my account is offered through my employer, who pays the fees? Me? My employer? Can I pay fees directly or do they have to be paid from my account?**
  If fees are charged against your account, it reduces the amount you have available to spend on health care. Part of the value of having an HSA is that unspent balances earn interest and can be invested over time.

Ask the Following Questions About Account Earnings

- **What is the rate of return on my account?**
  For instance, what interest rate does it earn, and how is it compounded?

- **What is the minimum balance threshold in order to make investments?**

- **Is there a charge to make investments or is there a minimum amount of money that must be invested?**

- **Are investment earnings on my account ever forfeitable? Does the account carry investment risk? Is it FDIC-insured?**
  Manage your HSA in the same careful way you manage any other investment.

Some Account Management Issues to Understand

- **Can my creditors seize balances in my HSA in the event I declare personal bankruptcy?**
  For more information about HSAs and bankruptcy,
  see "Chapter 11—HSA Laws and Health Care Reform".

- **Does the account trustee or custodian impose limits on the size or number of distributions I can take during a given period?**

- **Does the account trustee or custodian accept rollovers or trustee-to-trustee transfers from other eligible accounts?**
  Trustees and custodians may accept rollovers and transfers, but are not required to.

- **How easy is it to move money from an investment account back to the HSA if needed for a large medical expense? Is there a waiting period? Are there extra fees?**

Ask About Additional Services

Health care cost structures can be confusing. Prices are not always readily apparent. As an HSA owner, you want to maximize your investment and spend your money wisely.

Some forward-thinking HSA providers offer services to assist you in making smart choices. Make sure to find out if your potential HSA provider offers value-added services to help you better manage how to save and spend your health care dollars.

- **Will I have access to quality and cost comparison tools from my employer, health plan or HSA custodian?**
- **Does the account trustee or custodian provide phone and/or online help to assist me in reviewing and minimizing my health care spending?**
- **When is phone support available? What if I have an emergency in the middle of the night?**

Opening the Account

You can open your HSA any time of the year, as long as you are already enrolled in a qualified HDHP. Most people enroll in their HSAs during their employer's yearly benefits open enrollment period.

Where to Enroll

In most cases, you will go to your employee benefits or HR website to enroll online.

If you are opening your account independent of your employer, the HSA provider you select should have an easy-to-use online enrollment process.

If you are opening an HSA at a regular bank, you can enroll in person or on the bank's website.

Your insurance broker will also have forms or web sites to help you enroll in an HSA.

Signing a Custodial Agreement

Your HSA provider will require you to sign a custodial agreement and a trust agreement, or otherwise enroll as part of your employer-based health insurance program.

Some HSA administrators do not require "wet signatures," or paper forms if the enrollment process is tied to enrolling for the HDHP. In that case, you can enroll online at the same time you enroll in your insurance plan.

The IRS prototype forms for HSA custodial accounts (5305-C) and HSA trust accounts (5305-B) can be found on the IRS web site at www.irs.gov.

Designating a Beneficiary

Once your HSA is set up, you should designate a beneficiary. If your beneficiary is your spouse, he or she will become the owner of the HSA if you die. The HSA will be included in your estate for other named beneficiaries.

Receiving Your Welcome Kit, Debit Card, and/or Checkbook

Once your HSA is open, you will typically receive a debit card and/or checkbook from your HSA administrator. Doctor visits remain the same, except you may be required to pay at the time of service.

If your HDHP is a network plan and you use its providers, your bill may be sent to your insurance company first for repricing, and then be returned to you for payment at a discounted rate.

Ask your health care provider to contact your health plan for claim submission information. Your HSA administrator and your health plan can assist you if you have questions.

- Obtain your debit card and/or checkbook.
- Keep track of your account as you would your bank and retirement accounts.

Learning More about HSAs

There are a number of good web sites that describe the basics of HSAs, give updates about changes in HSA law, and list companies that provide HSAs.

Below is a list of some of these sites:

www.healthequity.com

www.healthcare.gov

www.hsafinder.com

www.treasury.gov

www.ehealth.com

www.devenir.com

CHAPTER 4

Contributing to Your HSA

Who Can Contribute to Your HSA?

Anyone (employer, family member, or any other person) may contribute to an HSA on behalf of an eligible HSA holder.

Even state governments are able to make HSA contributions on behalf of eligible individuals who are insured under health plans or state high-risk pools that qualify as HDHPs.

Who Gets the Tax Breaks?

HSA contributions are tax-deductible, grow tax-free, and are never taxed if used for qualified medical expenses. However, only you and your employer can claim a tax deduction when a contribution to your account is made.

Others who contribute to your account are unable to take a tax deduction. However, it is not required that their contributions toward your HSA count toward your gross income. In other words, all contributions to your HSA, no matter what the source, are tax-free to you.

HSAs are funded on a pre-tax basis. For an individual, it is an above-the-line deduction, independent of whether or not you itemize.

Employer contributions are not taxable to the employee, nor are they subject to employment taxes, such as Social Security payroll taxes or the federal portion of taxes that finance unemployment benefits. The earned income tax credit (EITC) isn't affected by employer contributions.

Self-employed individuals and owners of S corporations are not considered employees. As such, they cannot receive employer contributions. However, they can make contributions on their own, and claim the above-the-line deduction on their personal income taxes.

Contributions made by an individual are taken as a deduction on form 1040, and you are therefore not required to itemize in order to receive the tax break. Your employer will report the employer HSA contributions on your Form W-2, and your HSA trustee or custodian will report distributions to you and the IRS on Form 1099-SA.

Who Owns the HSA and All of the Contributions?

HSA dollars are owned by you, the account holder, and cannot be taken by the employer's creditors in the event of a company lawsuit or company bankruptcy.

Unused money rolls over to the next year and is fully portable. This means you take it with you in the event that you leave your employer, your employer changes health plans, or you change your health plan.

An account beneficiary's interest in an HSA is not forfeitable, so an employer cannot recoup any contribution previously made to your HSA.

Example

Employee Quits Before Completing a Full Year of Employment

Ken's employer contributed $2,000 to his HSA on January 1, 2014 expecting that he would work through December 31.

Ken terminated his employment on May 3, 2014.

His employer may not recoup any portion of its contribution to Ken's HSA.

Yearly Contribution Limits

The maximum amount you can contribute to your HSA is determined by the IRS. All HSA holders with a qualified plan may contribute up to these limits.

The limit for individuals in 2014 is $3,300 and the limit for families is $6,550. Individuals age 55 and older can make an additional annual catch-up contribution of $1,000.

The following table shows the maximum allowed contribution limits for a total contribution (from all sources) over a year, though HSA holders and employers can contribute less if desired:

HSA Contribution Limit	2014
Individual	$3,300
Family	$6,550
Additional catch-up contribution for those 55+	$1,000

The same annual contribution limit applies regardless of who contributes. These contribution limits are set by law, and are updated each year to allow for inflation.

Example

An Employer Contributes to an Employee's HSA

Jerome and Taneesha are married and have a qualified HDHP with a family deductible of $3,500 effective January 1, 2014.

Jerome's employer contributes $85 per month to his HSA, for a total of $1,020 per year.

Jerome's maximum 2014 HSA contribution limit is $6,550, so he can personally contribute up to an additional $5,530.

He can also choose to deposit less, or nothing into his account.

Catch-Up Contributions for Individuals 55 Years of Age and Older

For individuals 55 and older, contributions can be made that are higher than the limit. These are called catch-up contributions.

Similar to an IRA, the money in HSAs can roll over from year-to-year. Like IRA owners, HSA owners age 55 and older can contribute more, in hopes of boosting the savings in their HSA. These catch-up amounts are as follows:

- 2013: $1,000
- 2014: $1,000

Catch-Up Contributions for Spouses

If each spouse is 55 or older, they must both have individual HSAs in order for each to make a catch-up contribution. A married couple with two HSAs may make catch-up contributions totaling $2,000 in 2013 and 2014.

All contributions must cease once an individual enrolls in Medicare, as they are then no longer in an HSA-qualified health plan. (However, they can continue to invest the money and take distributions for qualified medical expenses).

If the account holder becomes eligible after January 1, the individual can choose to contribute the entire catch-up contribution. In order to do so, the individual must remain eligible for the remainder of that year, as well as the entire 12-month testing period following that year.

If the account holder does not remain eligible during that period of time, both years must be prorated and the excess contribution removed. The excess amount will be included as income for tax purposes, and an additional 10% tax applies.

Example

Married Couple Making Catch-Up Contributions

If Roger and Noelle are both older than 55 and neither is covered by Medicare, they can contribute an additional $2,000 ($1,000 each) to their individual HSAs for 2013 and 2014.

If only Roger has an HSA, he can contribute an extra $1,000 as a catch-up contribution.

More Options at Age 65 and After

If you choose to enroll in Medicare at the age of 65 or older, you may still use your HSA for health care expenses. However, you will not be allowed to make contributions, as you are no longer enrolled in a qualified HDHP.

Rather, if you decide to delay your enrollment in Medicare, you can continue to make contributions past the age of 65, as long as you are still covered by an HSA-qualified HDHP. In addition, you can also continue to make $1,000 yearly catch-up contributions.

Opening an HSA Mid-Year

New account holders who join an HDHP and open an HSA mid-year have two choices:

- Contribute a prorated amount for the actual number of months they are eligible during the year, or
- Take advantage of the IRS full-contribution rule and contribute the entire yearly maximum for their age and level of coverage

Prorating the Maximum Yearly Contribution

If you are not certain you will still be enrolled in your HDHP during the entire next tax year, you can contribute a prorated amount for the months you are actually eligible in the current tax year.

To do this, divide the yearly allowable maximum contribution by 12, then multiply the result by the number of months you're eligible during that tax year.

Example

Contributing a Prorated Amount for a Partial Year of Eligibility

Carlos started a new job in September and enrolled in a qualified HDHP on October 1, 2014.

He was told that his assignment will not be considered permanent until the end of his company's standard six-month probationary period.

Carlos wants to contribute as much as possible to his HSA, but there are only three months left in the year and he has no guarantee that he will be employed and covered by his HDHP the entire following year.

Carlos decides to prorate his contribution for the months he is actually enrolled in the HDHP in the current year.

He divides his yearly maximum contribution by 12 (1/12 of $3,300 = $275).

The prorated amount that Carlos can contribute for the current year is three months x $275, or $825.

Contributing Under the Full-Contribution Rule

Under the full-contribution rule, if you are an eligible individual on the first day of the last month of your tax year (December 1 for most taxpayers), you are considered to be an eligible individual for the entire year. You are treated as having the same HDHP coverage for the entire year, as you had on the first day of that last month.

- If you have single-only HDHP coverage, you can contribute the entire $3,300 for 2014. If you are 55 years of age or older, you can also contribute the entire catch-up contribution of $1,000, for a total of $4,300 for 2014.

- If you have family HDHP coverage, you can contribute the entire $6,550 for 2014 (plus the annual catch-up contribution if you are 55 or older).

Remaining Eligible During the Testing Period

If contributions were made to your HSA based on your eligibility for the entire year under the full-contribution rule, you must remain an eligible individual during the testing period.

For the full-contribution rule, the testing period begins with the last month of your tax year and ends on the last day of the 12th month following that month. For example, December 1, 2013, through December 31, 2014.

If you fail to remain an eligible individual during the testing period, other than because of death or disability, you have to include as income the total contributions made to your HSA that would not have been made except for the last-month rule. You must include this amount in your income in the year during which you fail to be an eligible individual. This amount is also subject to a 10% additional tax. The income and additional tax are shown on IRS Form 8889, Part III.

Example

Making a Maximum Contribution Late in the Calendar Year—Then Leaving the HDHP Early

Sixty-year-old Lian started a new job and enrolled in her HDHP and HSA on June 1, 2014.

Because she planned to retire in five years, she wanted to build all of her retirement accounts as quickly as possible. She decided to take advantage of the full-contribution rule and deposit the maximum yearly amount in her HSA ($3,300 plus her catch-up contribution of $1,000 = $4,300).

Because she started her new job on June 1, Lian was in a qualified HDHP for only seven months in 2014.

Lian knew she would need to remain in a qualified HDHP until December 31, 2015 to avoid taxes and penalties on the extra amount she contributed in 2014.

Unfortunately, Lian's employer layed her off in March 2015.

Lian realized that because she did not stay in her employer's HDHP during the entire testing period (Dec. 1, 2014 through Dec. 31, 2015), she would have to pay income tax and 10% additional tax on the amount she over-contributed for 2014.

To see what she would have to pay, she divided the amount she contributed in 2014 by 12 to get the prorated monthly amount.

$4,300/12 = $358.33

Then, she multiplied the monthly prorated amount by five to get the amount she overcontributed for the five months when she was not enrolled in an HDHP in 2014.

5 x $358.33 = $1,791.65

She prepared to add the $1,791.65 to her adjusted gross income on her 2015 tax return and pay an additional 10% tax ($179.17).

Example (cont.)

The Better Ending

Wisely, Lian talked to a tax adviser as soon as she was laid off. The tax adviser told her that continuing her HDHP coverage under COBRA until December 31, 2014 would satisfy the testing period.

The tax adviser gave Lian more good news. The law allowed Lian to use her HSA funds to pay the COBRA premiums.

Not only did she avoid the tax and penalty, she also had continued health insurance coverage throughout the rest of 2014, even though she was still unemployed.

Lian could afford the COBRA premiums because she had maximized her HSA balance, and because the COBRA premiums for an HDHP plan are lower than for a traditional low-deductible health plan.

When Can Contributions Be Made?

Eligibility Is Determined on a Monthly Basis

Eligibility to contribute to an HSA is determined on a monthly basis.

- Participants must be enrolled in a qualified HDHP on the first day of the month in order to make or receive an HSA contribution during that month.
- Unless you are contributing under the full-contribution rule (see the previous section), you cannot make HSA contributions for the months you are not covered by an HDHP.

Contributions Are Tied to the Tax Year

Contributions are reported on the individual tax return and therefore are tied to the tax return for that year. Consequently, the contribution may not be made before the beginning of the tax year that it covers and must be made no later than the legal deadline, without extensions, for filing the individual's income tax return for that year.

Most individuals are calendar-year taxpayers. For such individuals, contributions can be made between January 1 of a given year and April 15 of the following year.

Even though your health coverage plan year may be any 12-month period established by an employer or insurer for managing the plan and accounting for benefit payments, the schedule for HSA contributions aligns with the tax year.

Timing of Contributions

You have a lot of flexibility in deciding when to make your contributions. You and your employer can make your contributions in one or more payments at any time of the year, according to your convenience.

Example

Front Loading the HSA Early in the Year

Miles and Donetta knew their first baby was going to be born early in the year with a gastrointestinal defect that would probably require him to spend his first few weeks in the neonatal intensive care unit.

The hospital told them that they would be responsible for paying their entire out-of-pocket maximum on a payment plan with a high interest rate. If they did not have enough money in their HSA, they would be making those payments with post-tax dollars.

Donetta and the baby were healthy enough that she could keep working until a month before the baby's birth.

She and Miles decided to have her entire paycheck deposited into their HSA. When they had contributed up to the $6,550 family limit for 2014, they stopped the HSA payroll deductions.

When the baby was born, they paid their deductible and coinsurance out of the HSA until their out-of-pocket maximum was met. Then their HDHP paid 100% of their remaining expenses.

Miles calculated their tax savings and the credit interest rates they avoided. He estimated that their actual out-of-pocket expense was much lower than it would have been had they been enrolled in their previous traditional low-deductible, PPO plan.

Transfers from Other Tax-Advantaged Accounts

Transferring an HSA from One Trustee to Another

Trustee-to-trustee transfers are transfers of account balances directly from one trustee or custodian to another.

Transfers from other HSAs or from Archer MSAs into an HSA are permitted, as long as you are the owner of both accounts.

You may not transfer money from another individual's HSA—even if they are a family member or spouse—into an HSA in your name.

HSA transfers of balances accumulated in previous tax years do not affect the current year's contribution limits. This type of transfer is similar to moving funds from one IRA to another.

There is no limit to the number of trustee-to-trustee transfers you can make within a 12-month period.

Rollover Contributions from Another HSA or MSA

Rollover contributions are moving the funds from one HSA or Archer MSA to another, but the funds are sent to the account holder rather than directly from one trustee/custodian to another. The individual has 60 days to get the funds back into an HSA without incurring taxes or penalties.

Only one rollover can be completed in a 12-month period. Just like trustee-to-trustee transfers, the rollover does not apply toward the contribution limits for the year.

Example

Transferring an HSA to Another Bank or Trustee

Tyler has an HSA with $5,000 at Bank A and wishes to transfer the entire account to an HSA at Bank B.

He can rollover his money by withdrawing the balance from Bank A and re-depositing it in Bank B, as long as it is done within 60 days (he may also request a trustee-to-trustee transfer, in which Bank A sends the money directly to Bank B).

Tyler may choose either of these options and still make whatever contributions he is eligible to make for that tax year, without having to consider the rolled over amount in his yearly limit calculations.

However, if Tyler withdraws the money and does not re-deposit it or spend it for qualified health care within 60 days, a 20% penalty will apply and he will have to pay income tax on the amount.

IRA Transfers

To help fund the HSA, an account holder can do a once-per-lifetime trustee-to-trustee transfer from a traditional or Roth IRA to the HSA. This transfer is limited to the maximum annual contribution for the year and reduces the annual amount that can be contributed.

The individual must remain an eligible individual for the entire 12-month testing period following the month the transfer is completed. If he or she does not remain eligible, the transferred amount is included as income for tax purposes and is assessed an additional 10% penalty.

Simple and SEP IRAs are not eligible for transfer.

Contributions by Spouses

An HSA is an individual account only. Even when a husband and wife work for the same employer, their HSAs and contributions must be separate. Spouses cannot roll over their HSAs into a joint account.

The rules for married people apply only if both spouses are eligible individuals. Contribution limits for spouses depend on the kind of coverage each spouse chooses.

- If either spouse has family HDHP coverage, both spouses are treated as having family HDHP coverage.
- If each spouse has family coverage under a separate plan, the contribution limit for the two of them combined is $6,550 in 2014. The contribution limit is split equally between the spouses, unless they agree on a different division.
- If both spouses are 55 or older and not enrolled in Medicare, each spouse's contribution limit is increased by the $1,000 catch-up contribution. If both spouses meet the age requirement, the total contributions under family coverage cannot be more than $8,550 ($6,550 + $1,000 + $1,000) in 2014. Each spouse must make the catch-up contribution to his or her own HSA.

Example

Both Spouses Have Family Coverage

Tom, 58, and Alice, 53, are married.

Tom and Alice each have family coverage under a separate HDHP.

Because both plans provide family coverage, Tom and Alice are treated as having coverage under one family plan.

If they decide to split the $6,550 maximum family contribution for 2014 equally, Tom can contribute $3,275 to his HSA (half of the annual statutory amount of $6,550 for 2014, plus a $1,000 catch-up contribution because he is over 55).

Alice can contribute $3,275 to her HSA (half of the $6,550 annual maximum for a family). Being only 53, she is not eligible to make an additional catch-up contributions.

Tom and Alice can agree to contribute different amounts, but their total annual 2014 contributions cannot exceed $7,550 ($6,550 + $1,000).

Example

Both Spouses Have Self-Only Coverage

Jim, 35, and Kathy, 33, are married. Each has a self-only HDHP, and each has an HSA.

Jim can contribute $3,300 to his HSA in 2014, and Kathy can contribute $3,300 to hers.

The same applies whether Jim and Kathy work for different employers, one is self-employed and one is an employee, or both are self-employed.

Example

One Spouse Has Qualifying Coverage, the Other Does Not

David and Sherry are married.

David's employer offers an HSA-qualified HDHP.

Sherry's employer offers a traditional PPO plan that does not meet eligibility requirements for an HDHP.

Sherry elects family coverage, thereby covering David under her non-qualifying plan. David is not eligible to contribute to an HSA, because he is covered under Sherry's traditional plan.

However, if Sherry elected coverage under her plan for solely herself or their children included, David would not be covered under her plan. He could participate in his employer's HSA-qualified HDHP instead.

Example

One Spouse Is Eligible to Open an HSA, the Other Is Not

Joe, 65, and Jenny, 56, are married. Joe just turned 65 and enrolled in Medicare.

Joe and Jenny have separate HSAs, each with self-only coverage.

Joe can no longer contribute to his HSA, but can continue to use the funds accumulated in his account or Jenny's account to pay qualified medical expenses, including his Medicare premiums (except Medigap).

Jenny is enrolled in a qualified HDHP. She is eligible to contribute up to $3,300 to her HSA in 2014, plus a catch-up contribution of $1,000, because she is older than 55.

Example

Family and Single Coverage at the Same Time

Al and Sue are married.

Because he has young children from a previous marriage, Al has a family HDHP with a $5,000 deductible. Through her employer, Sue has a self-only HDHP with a $2,000 deductible.

Because one spouse has a family HDHP that could potentially cover the other spouse, they are seen as having family coverage. Their maximum combined contribution is the IRS statutory amount for family coverage—$6,550 for 2014, to be divided between them by agreement.

They file separate tax returns. Because she has no children of her own to claim as deductions like Al does, they determine that they could save the most on taxes if Sue makes a larger contribution toward the HSA. They decide that Sue will contribute 75% of the yearly maximum HSA contribution for their family ($4,912.50), and Al will contribute 25% ($1,637.50).

Contributions by an Individual or a Sole Proprietor

Sole Proprietors are treated the same as individuals who make their own HSA contributions. They can deduct their own HSA contributions and health insurance payments from their personal income tax returns.

Sole proprietors cannot deduct their own HSA contributions as a business expense. However, amounts contributed on behalf of their employees may be deductible on Schedule C. The owner's HSA contribution is not a deduction attributable to the self-employed individual's trade or business, so it is not taken as a deduction on Schedule C, nor is it taken into account in determining net earnings from self-employment on Schedule SE.

Contributions by a Partnership and Multiple Member LLCs*

Contributions from a partnership to a partner's HSA are not contributions by an employer. The contributions are treated as a distribution of money to the partner.

Contributions from a partner to an HSA in exchange for services rendered are treated as guaranteed payments. They can be deducted by the partner and are included in the partner's gross income.

In both situations, the partner can deduct the contribution made to the HSA.

Contributions by an S Corporation

Contributions by an S corporation to a >2% shareholder/employee's HSA for services rendered are treated as guaranteed payments, are deducted by the S corporation, and are included in the shareholder-employee's gross income. The shareholder employee can deduct the contribution made to the shareholder/employee's HSA on his or her personal income tax return.

*Single member LLCs are treated the same as sole proprietors.

Penalties for Contributing Too Much to Your HSA

Excess Contribution

If you contribute more than the allowable amount to your HSA during the year and you have not used the full-contribution rule, it is called an excess contribution. Excess contributions are included in income and subject to a 6% excise tax. Excess employer contributions also become subject to income and excise tax.

You can avoid paying the excise tax and withdraw some or all of the excess contributions if you meet the following conditions:

- You withdraw the excess contributions by the due date of your tax return for the year the contributions were made.
- You withdraw any income earned on the withdrawn contributions and include the earnings in "other income" on your tax return for the year you withdraw the contributions and earnings.

Failing the Testing Period under the Full-Contribution Rule

If you used the full-contribution rule to make a full year's allowable contribution to your HSA, but did not fulfill the testing period, the penalty is a 10% tax, plus income tax on the over-contribution.

If you find out that you will not meet the testing period before the tax filing deadline for the previous year, you can follow the steps for withdrawing excess contributions in the section above.

If you lose your eligibility after the previous year's tax filing deadline, you must follow the steps earlier in the chapter under the section, "Contributing Under the Full-Contribution Rule" to calculate the additional tax you will need to pay on your over-contribution.

Calculating Penalties for Excess Contributions

The most reliable way to determine your tax liability for excess contributions is to download IRS Form 5329 and its instructions from www.irs.gov and use the form as a worksheet.

CHAPTER 5

Using and Growing Your HSA

Whose Expenses Can Your HSA Cover?

Under the law, HSA distributions are tax-free if used for qualified medical expenses for:

- You and your spouse
- Any dependents you claim on your tax return
- Any person you could have claimed as a dependent

Whose Expenses Does Your HSA Cover?

Under the law, HSA distributions are tax-free if used for qualified medical expenses for:

- **You and your spouse**
  This is true whether or not your spouse or dependent is covered by an HDHP. Even if both spouses have an HSA, one spouse can pay for qualified medical expenses for the other.

- **Any dependents you claim on your tax return**
  According to IRS Publication 502, a person you claim as a dependent for income tax purposes must meet each of the following criteria:

  1. Lived with you for the entire year as a member of your household or is:

  - Your child (including a legally adopted or foster child), grandchild, or great-grandchild
  - Your stepchild or your stepchild's descendant
  - Your sibling, half-sibling, step-sibling, or a descendant of these
  - Your parent, grandparent, or other direct blood ancestor
  - Your stepfather or stepmother
  - A brother or sister of your father or mother
  - A descendant of your brother or sister
  - Your father-in-law, mother-in-law, son-in-law, daughter-in-law, brother-in-law, or sister-in-law

  2. The person was a US citizen or resident, or a resident of Canada or Mexico for some part of the calendar year during which your tax year began (for individual taxpayers, the tax year is typically the calendar year).

  3. You provided more than half of that person's total support for the calendar year (special rules may apply to children for divorces and other situations).

  4. You may claim a child who meets one of the tests in No. 1 above as your dependent, if he/she lived with you in the U.S. (special rules may apply) for more than half of the year and is under 19 (or under 24 if a full-time student).

5. Check with your tax professional for your children if they are permanently and totally disabled.

- **Any person you could have claimed as a dependent on your return except when:**

1. The person filed a joint return

2. The person had a gross income of $3,700 or more

3. You or your spouse, if filing jointly, can be claimed as a dependent on someone else's return

Example

Paying Expenses for a Spouse Who Is Not Covered by the HDHP

Sherry has a traditional plan that does not meet the criteria for an HDHP and does not cover David, her husband.

Sherry's plan has first-dollar coverage that is subject to co-payments. David elects an HDHP/HSA for himself.

Even though Sherry is not covered by David's HDHP, he can use his HSA to pay for her co-payments.

Multiple Definitions of Dependent

The uses of the word dependent in PPACA (Health Care Reform Law) and in the IRS tax code are not the same. Health plans and state laws add to the confusion with their own rules for dependents.

For making qualified distributions from an HSA, a dependent is defined by the Internal Revenue Code (IRC), section 152, and is explained in more detail in the previous section.

Adult Children Up to Age 26

PPACA requires that health plans offer coverage for adult children up to age 26 under a parent's family health plan. While they may qualify as a dependent for insurance purposes, adult children might not qualify as tax dependents on the parent's tax return. If that is the case, their medical expenses cannot be covered by a parent's HSA.

However, an adult child who is covered under a parent's family HSA-eligible HDHP can open his or her own HSA and contribute up to the full family maximum.

Domestic Partners and Same-Sex Spouses

HSAs can be used to pay medical expenses of domestic partners and same-sex spouses only when the partner is the HSA owner's qualified tax dependent under IRC section 152. See also IRC section 223(d)(2)(A).

Paying for Qualified Medical Expenses

Your HSA can be used for a wide variety of medical expenses, including those which are deducted from your individual tax return if you are eligible (see Appendix C for a detailed list of qualified medical expenses).

Any money from the HSA used for non-medical purposes will be included in the individual's gross income for tax purposes and is subject to an additional 20% penalty on the amount included. However, if the account holder or beneficiary reaches the age of 65 or dies, distributions may be used for other purposes without being subject to the penalty. Income taxes will still apply.

When Do Expenses Have to Be Incurred?

Only expenses incurred after you establish your HSA are considered qualified. Expenses incurred before you establish your HSA are not qualified medical expenses.

When Is an HSA Established?

Under federal law, you cannot open an HSA and incur qualified expenses until the first day of the month after you enroll in a qualified HDHP (if you enroll in your HDHP on the first day of a month, you can open your HSA that same day).

State law determines when an HSA is established. In most cases, it is as soon as you complete your account application, pass the Consumer Identity Program (CIP) verification required by the Patriot Act, and fund your account.

An HSA that is funded by amounts rolled over from an Archer MSA or other HSA is established on the date the prior account was established.

If, under the full-contribution rule, you are considered eligible for the entire year for determining the contribution amount, only those expenses incurred after you establish your HSA are qualified medical expenses.

Some state laws have determined that an HSA is deemed open on the first day that the tax payers are considered covered by a qualified HDHP. Check with your tax professional for more details.

IRS Definition of Qualified Medical Expenses

Appendix C has a detailed list of qualified medical expenses. Here are some general guidelines from IRS Publication 502:

- Medical expenses are the costs of diagnosis, cure, mitigation, treatment, or prevention of disease, and the costs for treatments affecting any part or function of the body.

  These expenses include payments for legal medical services rendered by physicians, surgeons, dentists, and other medical practitioners. They also include the costs of equipment, supplies, and diagnostic devices needed for these purposes.

- Medical care expenses must be primarily used to alleviate or prevent a physical or mental defect or illness. They do not include expenses that are merely beneficial to general health, such as vitamins (unless prescribed) or a vacation.

- Medical expenses include the premiums for long-term care insurance, COBRA premiums, and insurance premiums paid during periods of unemployment. Other long-term care expenses, beyond premiums, can also be paid from an HSA.

Paying for Some Insurance Premiums

Generally, you cannot use your HSA to pay medical insurance premiums, but there are some exceptions.

Medicare Premiums

Once you are 65 and eligible for Medicare, you can use your HSA to pay Medicare premiums (A, B, C, and D), out-of-pocket expenses that Medicare does not pay, and Medicare HMO premiums.

You cannot pay Medigap premiums with your HSA. Medigap is insurance that individuals can buy to cover out-of-pocket costs that are not covered by Medicare.

Premiums for Employer-Based Coverage After Age 65

If you are 65 or older and still working, you can pay your share of premiums for employer-based coverage out of your HSA (you cannot pay for these premiums before age 65).

If you are 65 or older and not working, you can pay your share of any premiums your employer requires you to pay for employer-sponsored retiree health care coverage.

Premiums When You Are Unemployed

You can pay for health care coverage while receiving unemployment compensation under federal or state law.

You can also pay COBRA premiums with HSA dollars if you are eligible for COBRA benefits.

Long-Term Care Insurance

You can also use your HSA to pay premiums for qualified long-term care insurance. To be qualified, a long-term care insurance plan must meet criteria determined by federal law (see IRS Publication 969).

Restrictions Your HSA Trustee or Custodian May Impose

It is your responsibility to prove you have spent your HSA funds in accordance with the law. However, the trustee or custodian can limit your access to HSA distributions under certain conditions.

For example, the trustee may prohibit distributions for amounts less than $50, or may only allow a certain number of distributions.

Trustees and custodians may impose different restrictions (including no restrictions at all), on distributions. If easy access to your account is important to you, consider this feature when shopping for an HSA.

Paying for Services Covered Under Your Health Plan

In general, the HSA-qualified HDHP combination is the most flexible type of health care arrangement available. The money in the HSA is yours to spend and save. This means you can choose to obtain treatment from virtually any licensed provider of qualified medical services, whether they are in or out of your network, as long as you are willing to pay with your HSA.

Using Network Providers

Your HSA money typically goes further if you take advantage of the discounts provided by your health plan's network.

Health care providers—doctors, hospitals, and other health care facilities—participating in your plan's network are those that have agreed to give members of your plan a discount on their usual charges.

Depending on your plan's rules, you may also need to use a gatekeeper, or primary care physician, and/or obtain referrals and authorizations for certain medical services or procedures in order to get the best benefits your plan offers.

A gatekeeper physician is usually a primary care doctor, pediatrician, or internist responsible for overseeing and coordinating all aspects of a patient's care.

A referral is a recommendation from one physician to see another physician, usually a specialist. In many managed care plans, in order for the service to be covered, a referral may be necessary to see any practitioner or specialist other than your gatekeeper physician.

An authorization is the health plan's permission to proceed with a medical or surgical procedure. Like a referral, an authorization may be required if you want the plan to pay for the procedure. Without authorization, the plan may refuse to pay for the procedure, even if the procedure might have otherwise been covered.

A managed care plan is a health plan that limits the reimbursement levels paid to providers by monitoring health care utilization of participants.

If you use your HSA only for services covered under your plan and consult only providers who participate in your plan's network, all of your expenditures under the HSA will generally count toward your deductible and toward your plan's out-of-pocket limits.

Example

Paying a Network Provider

Maria's doctor charges $150 for a visit for an acute sore throat.

As a provider in her plan's network, her doctor has agreed to accept $75 from her plan for this type of visit.

Maria does not pay her provider the $150 charge at the time of the visit. Because her provider is in her plan's network, she waits for the claim to show up on her HSA provider's website after the health plan applies the discount that her provider agreed to accept. She may also receive a bill directly from her doctor for the adjusted amount.

If she has not yet met her deductible at the time of the visit, she pays the $75 out of her HSA or out of her other savings with post-tax dollars.

This amount is also credited toward her plan's annual out-of-pocket limit, or limit on how much she can be expected to spend in a given year before the plan takes over entirely.

Even if you use network providers, you still need to understand exactly how your plan expects you to obtain care. Your plan may require you to obtain a referral to see a specialist or authorization for a medical procedure, even if the specialist or the doctor recommending the procedure participates in your plan.

If you fail to obtain a referral or authorization when one is required, your plan may charge you a higher co-payment, coinsurance rate, or a flat-dollar penalty. The excess co-payments, coinsurance, or penalties for not using network providers will not count toward your HDHP's out-of-pocket limit for the year, however, you will be able to pay these out of your HSA.

Failure to know and follow your plan's rules can cost you money.

Separate Out-of-Pocket Limits for Out-of-Network Care

HSA law permits health plans to have separate out-of-pocket limits for out-of-network care.

Refusal of Charges

If your provider has not contracted with your plan, the plan is not obligated to accept the provider's full charges.

Plans typically count only what they consider usual, customary, and reasonable (UCR). UCR is the estimated "going rate" paid in your geographical area for a given medical service or procedure. This amount is credited toward the participant's deductible and/or out-of-pocket limits.

Example

Only a Portion of a Provider's Fees Applied to the Deductible

Maria's doctor charges $150 for a sore throat evaluation. Her insurance company decides that the usual and customary charge is $130. It then pays half of this reduced amount.

Maria pays the remaining half, and possibly an additional $20 if the doctor does not have a previous agreement to accept the plan's reduced charges and passes them on to Maria directly.

If this happens, Maria's cost for the visit is $85. The doctor still gets paid his usual charge of $150—$85 from Maria and $65 from her insurance company.

However, because her insurance company has not allowed the full amount of her doctor's charges to be considered, only $65 of the $85 she paid is credited toward her deductible and out-of-pocket limit for the year.

Paying for Services Not Covered Under Your Health Plan

You can use your HSA balance to pay for health care not covered under your health plan within the limits of qualified expenses. This includes many dental and vision expenses, as well as many less-common expenses, such as removing lead-based paint from your residence.

However, because removing lead-based paint is an expense that would generally not be covered by a health insurance plan, that kind of expense would not be applied toward your health plan deductible. See Appendix C for more details.

Methods of Payment from an HSA

The basic process of paying for care under an HSA is much the same as it is under other health care plans.

Traditional Plan

In a traditional plan, you typically pay for care in one of two ways, depending on whether the doctor or other provider participates in your plan's network.

- **In-network care:** If the provider participates in your network, you typically present your health care plan membership card and pay the required co-payment at the time of the visit.

  The provider files your claim with the insurance company and gets paid the contractually agreed or repriced amount. If there is also coinsurance that is applicable to the service, then the provider bills you for the balance due.

- **Out-of-network care:** If the provider does not participate in your plan's network, the process is different. You pay the entire bill at the time of the visit, because an out-of-network provider typically will not submit the claim to your plan for you. Then you may be reimbursed by your insurance company for part of what you paid, depending on how much of your deductible, if any, you have met for the year.

HSA-Qualified HDHP

With an HSA-qualified HDHP, the payment process at the doctor's office (hospital, laboratory, or other facility) is similar.

Your HSA custodian may supply you with an HSA debit card and/or checkbook. Your HSA administrator may also provide an online bill pay service that lets you pay providers directly from your HSA.

- **In-network care:** If the doctor or other provider is in your network or the service is for preventative care, you may not have to pay anything at the time you receive care, depending on the structure of your plan.

  The provider may ask you to pay part of the bill at the time of your visit. If possible, do not pay the entire bill since it has not been re-priced and you might be overcharged. Also, remember that preventive care should be paid for by your health plan and not out of your HSA.

  After you have received care, the provider will submit your claim for repricing to the health plan. The health plan will pay its contractually agreed amount if you have met your deductible for the plan year. Additionally, the health plan takes into account whether you have a network discount, the claim is for preventive care, or you pay the reduced amount if you have not met your deductible.

  Depending on how your HSA is set up, you can pay your portion, if any, out of your bank account, with a credit card, file a claim for reimbursement from your HSA, or pay the amount directly out of your HSA using your HSA's online bill pay system.

- **Out-of-network care:** If your provider does not participate in your plan's network, you may have to pay at the time the care is provided. This also happens in a traditional plan. You can pay the charge out of your bank account or with a credit card and file a claim for reimbursement request from your HSA, or pay the amount directly out of your HSA using your HSA debit card or check.

  If you have overpaid the physician out of your HSA, you will receive a reimbursement that should be re-deposited into your HSA to avoid additional taxes.

Important Strategies for Managing Payments to Providers

While the basic outlines of the payment process are primarily the same whether you are enrolled in a traditional plan or in an HSA-qualified HDHP, it may be helpful to understand a few terms and to understand a few of the steps in the payment process.

Be Ready to Pay Co-Payments and Coinsurance or Encounter Fees

Most health care providers are not accustomed to cashless visits—where the patient is not expected to pay something at the time of the visit.

In a traditional plan, your co-payment or coinsurance serves as a down payment for care and the balance comes from your plan.

To accommodate the needs of providers, some HSA-qualified HDHPs may provide for an encounter fee, or an amount you pay at the time of a visit. While this fee may not represent your full financial responsibility to the provider, it is counted toward your financial responsibility for that visit and for your care for the year.

Try Not to Pay Retail Price for Visits

Important: Many providers, both in- and out-of-network, are unfamiliar with HSA-qualified HDHPs and will try to charge you retail price when you receive services. Speak with your HSA provider or health plan about the best way to obtain fair pricing when you visit your doctor.

Build Your HSA Early in the Year

The law governing HSAs provides you and/or your employer with a good amount of flexibility in funding your HSA. You or your employer can make contributions to the HSA on any schedule that is convenient, as long as the total contributions made to your account in a given year do not exceed the annual maximum contribution limit. Best of all, unlike most FSAs, funds in your HSA are not "use it or lose it", so you do not need to worry about over-contributing, provided you observe the maximum contribution limits.

If you have a bill that exceeds your balance, you can pay the bill using other resources, then file for reimbursement from your HSA once your balance has grown sufficiently. Your HSA trustee will provide you with forms or another process for getting reimbursements.

If your HSA is offered as part of a cafeteria plan, your employer may help you build up your HSA to meet your health care spending needs. If an employee elects to make contributions to an HSA through a cafeteria plan, the employer may contribute the maximum amount elected by the employee to the HSA.

This type of accelerated contribution must be equally available to all participating employees throughout the plan year and must be provided to all participating employees on the same terms. The employee then repays the advance or accelerated contribution through regularly scheduled cafeteria plan contributions.

Duplicate Reimbursements Must Be Returned to the HSA

If you pay directly from the HSA and then receive a duplicate reimbursement from the insurance company, the reimbursed amount must be returned to the HSA administrator as a mistaken distribution. If you do not return the duplicate reimbursement, you will have to pay a penalty to the IRS. This also applies to any refunds you receive from health providers for over-payment.

Mistaken distributions from an HSA can be repaid by April 15—or another date designated by the IRS—of the following year without penalty or tax, provided this is permitted by the trustee, and there is "convincing evidence that the amounts were distributed from an HSA because of a mistake of fact due to reasonable cause" (IRS Notice 2004-50 - Part III - Administrative, Procedural, and Misc.).

Investing Your HSA Funds

If you make your annual maximum contributions, are careful with your funds, and look for ways to get the best value (for example, comparing prescription prices at different pharmacies and usingin-network providers), the money will grow and earn interest over the years.

When your account balance reaches the minimum balance, if any, required by your HSA administrator for investing, you can invest any money over that threshold in HSA-qualified investment funds. Most HSA administrators provide a website that enables you to set up your investments and make trades.

Investment Choices

HSAs can be invested in the same investments approved for IRAs—i.e. bank accounts, annuities, certificates of deposit (CDs), stocks, mutual funds, or bonds. However, no part of the HSA trust assets can be invested in life insurance contracts, collectibles (art, antiques etc.—other tangible personal property that the IRS specifies), and HSA assets may not be co-mingled with other property except for investment purposes.

Earnings and Risk

Earnings on money invested from your HSA accrue tax-free. However, all investments carry the same risk as the stock market and mutual funds, and are not FDIC-insured.

Moving Funds Back Into Your HSA

If you have a large medical expense, you can move money out of your investments back into your HSA with no penalties and without affecting your yearly contribution maximum. If you choose an HSA administrator that offers no trading fees, you may also be able to make trades and maintain your investment account with no extra fees.

CHAPTER 6

Becoming a Smart Health Care Consumer

Getting the Most Out of Your HSA

As you become more educated about how your health plan works and ways to manage the features of your HSA, you will be able to stretch the dollars in your account to cover more health care needs, or better yet, earn more interest.

Put Premium Savings Into Your HSA

A higher deductible generally means lower monthly premiums. Take this into account when deciding whether or not to choose an HSA-qualified HDHP option.

While it may seem intimidating to take on a high deductible, an HDHP can cost significantly less. You can deposit all or some of your premium savings into your HSA. The balance in your account can be used to offset the higher deductible. If you do not need the money for medical expenses, it can grow. Unlike premium expenses and FSA contributions which are "use it or lose it," you get to keep your HSA dollars.

Compare Coinsurance and Co-Payment Levels

Another way to balance the benefits and risks of an HSA is to understand coinsurance levels. Coinsurance and co-payments determine what you pay once you and your family reach your plan's deductible.

Different coinsurance and co-payment levels can affect the premium price and the additional amount you may need to pay out of your HSA or out of pocket once the deductible is met.

For example, if your coinsurance level is 100% (your plan pays 100% after the deductible), your premium will most likely be higher than one with a coinsurance of 80/20 (the plan pays 80% and you pay 20% until you meet your out-of-pocket maximum). Most coinsurance levels will vary for in and out-of-pocket network care.

Take Advantage of Your HRA or FSA

Some employers offer limited-purpose HRAs to cover the gap between your deductible and the out-of-pocket maximum. Study the requirements for this benefit, keep good records of your expenses, and watch the calendar. Many people neglect to submit reimbursement requests to their employers before the FSA's or HRA's run-out deadline. Do not be one of them.

You may also have a limited-purpose FSA. During your open enrollment period, talk to your dentist and vision services provider to get an estimate of the dental and vision care you will need, then make an election for an FSA contribution to cover that amount. Make sure you do not over-contribute to the FSA, because you can lose any unspent money at the end of the year. Using an FSA for your dental and vision expenses instead of your HSA lets you stretch your HSA balance further. Limited purpose FSAs make the most sense for people that contribute the annual maximum to their HSA. You should always "top off" your HSA before contributing to your limited purpose FSA because HSA dollars can also be used for dental and vision but they are not "use it or lose it".

Watch Out-of-Pocket Maximums

Maximum out-of-pocket costs for health plans that qualify for HSA eligibility for individuals ($6,350 for 2014) and families ($12,700 for 2014) are set by the IRS for in-network care.

However, HDHP plans can have higher out-of-pocket maximums for out-of-network care. To reduce costs, be sure you know how much you will pay for out-of-network care before committing to it. Your out-of-pocket maximum level can affect your exposure and your ability to go out-of-network to receive expensive care.

Determine the Right Amount of Money to Contribute to Your HSA

Try to contribute the most money the law allows and that you are financially able to contribute to your HSA each year.

Why?

HSAs have the best tax benefits of any savings accounts, including traditional IRAs, 401(k)s, and Roth IRAs.

Only an HSA lets the owner make tax-deductible deposits, enjoy tax-free growth through interest or investments, and spend the money on qualified health-related services and products without paying taxes.

Unlike most other medical spending accounts such as FSAs or HRAs, the money in your HSA is yours to keep. It can also be used for non-health related costs by paying only your income tax, with no penalties when you reach 65.

Many people, including those with HSAs, may be on tight budgets and unable to fully fund the account. The good news is that the government allows you to increase or decrease your contributions throughout the year until April 15, or an IRS-adjusted date of the following year, and still receive tax benefits.

Funding strategies for HSAs and 401(k)s

Many employers are now offering their employees access to both 401(k)s and HSAs. Employees that fund both of these accounts should consider the unique "triple-tax advantaged" benefits of the HSA as they decide upon their funding strategy. You should consider funding these accounts in the following order:

1. Fund either or both accounts to optimize any available "employer matching contributions" that are available.
2. Fund the HSA to the allowable annual maximum.
3. Fund the 401(k) to the allowable annual maximum.

The main reasons for this order of funding is to benefit from employer matching funds while protecting your money from avoidable taxes. Remember, the HSA does not have FICA (social security) taxes on contributions and no taxes when you spend the dollars as long as it is on health care.

Use Payroll Deductions to Prefund Your Account for Anticipated Expenses

If you expect a large medical expense during the year, try to put your money into your HSA first through an increased payroll deduction, instead of paying directly out-of-pocket. That way, you can pay with pre-tax dollars. This increases the value of your money (depending on your tax bracket) by 18% to 30%.

You can also fully fund your HSA at the beginning of the year, provided you stay covered by a qualified HDHP for the entire year.

Example

Funding the HSA Early in the Year for an Anticipated Medical Expense

The Jensen family is expecting their second child in July, and their HDHP plan year began on January 1, 2014.

They have family coverage with a $5,000 deductible and no embedded deductible. Their plan has maternity coverage and no coinsurance once the deductible is met.

Expecting out-of-pocket expenses in July associated with the birth of their child, they increased their HSA contributions to $800 per month, so that by July 1, they will have deposited $4,800 in their HSA for the year.

For the 2014 tax year, the Jensens can deposit up to $6,550 into their account, so they can still contribute $1,750 over the next six months, assuming they remain eligible to contribute to the HSA for the entire year.

When they receive bills for the birth, they will have money in their HSA to satisfy up to $5,000 in bills.

Costs exceeding $5,000 will be fully paid by the HDHP, provided they remain in-network.

Consider Hospital Indemnity Plans and Other Gap Coverage

The HSA law allows you to use other types of insurance with your HDHP that can help offset the risk that comes with a higher deductible.

These policies include homeowner's insurance, automobile insurance, dental and vision care plans, accidental injury insurance, workers' compensation benefits, hospital indemnity plans that pay a fixed amount per day of hospitalization, and specific disease policies that pay a fixed amount for the designated disease.

The permitted plans help preserve your HSA balances and protect you from out-of-pocket expenses.

Become a Careful Shopper

The internet and your health plan should provide many opportunities to compare costs and shop for bargains on prescriptions and medical supplies. There are also some good websites that rate hospitals and compare costs of treatments. Your HSA administrator may provide links to cost comparison tools and websites on your HSA member portal. Spend time to become familiar with these resources.

The reference librarian at your local library is also a valuable ally for finding all possible resources for researching medical treatments, facilities, and costs.

You can also find suitable home-use alternatives to medications or supplies you usually get through your provider by comparison shopping at retail stores.

Example

Finding Bargains on Health Care

Holly, 35, is married and a mother of four. She was recently diagnosed with insulin-dependent diabetes.

Holly's husband recently left a job that offered health benefits through a low deductible, traditional plan. His new employer offers an HSA-qualified HDHP.

In Holly's words, "In a health insurance plan with a consistent co-payment of $10, I never had a reason to ask questions about the costs of services. I just paid the co-payment and felt grateful to have insurance pay the rest–or so I thought.

"Under my traditional HMO insurance plan, the pharmacy simply filled my prescriptions for my insulin and supplies, and I didn't see any need to look for more cost-effective prices. I was happy to pay my $35 co-payment for insulin.

"When introduced to health savings accounts, I was worried that I wouldn't get the same benefits. I learned though that not only did I receive comparable care, I also learned to be a careful shopper and save money.

"I began to ask questions about such things as lab work, blood tests, and examinations. I learned how to save money by switching to generic drugs and buying a less expensive blood glucose monitor and test strips. I found out that the typical blood work done at my doctor's office cost anywhere from $55 to $70.

"I found out that I could buy my own hemoglobin A1C test at my pharmacy for about $24. I did the test at home and called my doctor with the results. I also learned to watch for coupons and rebates.

"I've become more of a researcher for myself and for my children. Before taking them to the doctor or to the urgent care, I go online to learn what I can about their symptoms and possible treatments.

"I've discovered that by controlling my own medical dollars, I'm more conscientious about what I'm doing and spending, and we've saved money."

Case Studies

As you become familiar with the covered benefits, deductibles, contributions, and out-of-pocket expenses associated with your HDHP, you can begin to understand and plan for how to make your HSA work for you.

The following examples of real-life scenarios show how HSAs can help decrease insurance premiums and build good health care consumer skills. These studies illustrate how to get the most out of your HSA by:

- Understanding and selecting the best HDHP design for your situation.
- Determining the right amount of money to contribute to your HSA.

To make it easier to compare "Money In" versus "Money Out" in each of these case studies, the employee HSA contribution is $0.

Case Study 1:

Bill and Tammy—Some Chronic Illness

Bill and Tammy are middle-aged and starting to need care for chronic illnesses. During his employer's open enrollment period for 2014 benefits, Bill decides to use his and Tammy's medical history from 2013 to compare benefit options.

In 2013, Bill and Tammy took advantage of free preventive care screenings through their health plan. They were on regular medications for some mild chronic illness. They had only one urgent care visit during the year.

	Bill	Tammy
Age	58	57
Health	High cholesterol	Type 1 diabetic
Medications	Lipitor, 10 mg daily	Insulin, daily
Health Care Utilization	1 urgent care visit for cut hand Regular doctor and preventive visits	Regular doctor and preventive visits

The moment of truth came when Bill totaled the premiums, medical expenses, and his employer's contribution to the HSA.

Even though he did not meet the relatively high HDHP plan deductible and had to pay for medical expenses out of his HSA (and a little out of his own pocket after he depleted the HSA), the direct hit to his pocket was still $1,938 less under the HSA-qualified HDHP.

	PPO Plan		HDHP/HSA Plan	
Money In				
Employer HSA Contributions		$0	$125 x 12 months	$1,500
Money Out				
Annual Premiums	$275 x 12 months	$3,300	$125 x 12 months	$1,500
Total Provider Visits	Co-pays	$115	Paid from HSA	$895
Total Prescriptions	Co-pays	$140	Paid from HSA	$722
Money Out Subtotal		$3,555		$3,117
Less the HSA Employer Contribution		$0		-$1,500
Total Money Out		$3,555		$1,617
Difference between PPO and HDHP/ HSA Money Out				$1,938 savings
HSA Balance Remaining		$0		$0

Case Study 2:

Julie—Excellent Health

Julie knows the importance of health insurance and good habits. She watches what she eats and gets enough exercise and sleep.

She has a relatively low income, and she is very cost-sensitive.

	Julie
Age	35
Health	Excellent
Medications	1 generic prescription for strep
Health Care Utilization	2 doctor visits: Annual checkup Strep throat

Like Bill, Julie compares her two plan options using her expenses from 2013.

Julie is very concerned about the high deductible in the HSA-qualified HDHP. The $0 deductible in the PPO is very attractive to her. Even though she is in great health, she feels she cannot afford to cover unanticipated medical expenses. She does not have much money in her bank account at the end of each month.

She also sees that the out-of-pocket maximum for the HDHP is $3,000, compared to the $2,000 from the PPO plan.

Her employer is contributing $750 to her HSA, but she does not see much of an impact from that at first.

Insurance Plan

	PPO Plan		HDHP/HSA Plan	
Deductible		$0		$1,500
Out-of-Pocket Maximum		$2,000		$3,000
Annual Premiums	$85 x 12 months	$1,020	$25 x 12 months	$300
Employer HSA Contributions		$0	$62.50 x 12 months	$750
Employee HSA Contributions		n/a	$0 x 12 = $0	$0

Julie had her annual checkup, which was covered as a preventive benefit under her insurance plan.

Provider Visits

	PPO Plan		HDHP/HSA Plan	
2 annual preventive exams	Preventive covered at 100%	$0	Preventative covered at 100%	$0
1 $100 doctor visit for strep throat	$15 co-pay	$15	Pays from HSA	$100
Total Provider Costs		$15		$100

Case Study 2: (cont.)

Julie's only prescription in 2013 was a generic medication for strep throat.

Prescriptions

	PPO Plan		HDHP/HSA Plan	
1 $25 generic	$10 co-pay	$10	30% co-pay (Pays from HSA)	$7.50
Total Prescriptions		$10		$7.50

Everything comes into perspective when Julie compares "Money In" and "Money Out." Between the low premium and her employer's contribution to her HSA, she would be much better off with an HSA-qualified HDHP.

While she had been worried about a high deductible and a high out-of-pocket maximum, in reality she finished the year with a positive balance of more than $600 in her HSA. With its $0 deductible, the PPO plan would have taken over $700 more out of her pocket compared to the HSA plan when she counts monthly premiums and copay costs.

	PPO Plan		HDHP/HSA Plan	
Money In				
Employer HSA Contributions		$0	$62.50 x 12 months	$750
Money Out				
Annual Premiums	$85 x 12 months	$1,020	$25 x 12 months	$300
Total Provider Costs	Co-pays	$15	Paid from HSA	$100
Total Prescriptions	Co-pays	$10	Paid from HSA	$7.50
Total Money Out		$1,045		$342.50
Difference Between PPO and HDHP/HSA Money Out				$702.50 savings
HSA Balance Remaining		$0		$632.50

Case Study 3:

The Walkers—Excellent Health

The Walkers have two children. Derek works for an electrical contractor and Lauren works at a local university. She has better benefits, so the family is going to be covered by a family plan from her employer.

They have two very active, adventurous little boys. One was injured in a bicycle accident in 2013. They had no reason to expect that the boys would become more cautious in 2014.

	Derek	Lauren	2 Children
Age	38	36	10 and 6
Health	Excellent	Excellent	One child injured in a bicycle accident
Medications	None	None	None
Health Care Utilization	Regular doctor and preventive visits	Regular doctor and preventive visits	Regular doctor and preventive visits Hospital emergency room, surgery, and 3-day stay for injured child

Lauren compares her two 2014 plan options using the family's 2013 medical expenses as a guide. There is a PPO plan with a relatively low deductible and out-of-pocket maximum.

For family coverage, the HSA-qualified HDHP option has a higher deductible and out-of- pocket maximum.

Insurance Plan

	PPO Plan		HDHP/HSA Plan	
Deductible		$250		$2,500
Maximum Out-of-Pocket Limit		$2,500		$5,000
Coinsurance		20%		20%
Annual Premiums	$170.25 x 12 months	$2,043	$0 x 12 months	$0
Employer HSA Contributions		$0	$150 x 12 months	$1,800
Employee HSA Contributions		n/a	$0 x 12 = $0	$0

The hospital expenses for one of her little boys far exceeded the out-of-pocket maximum for both plans. So she just used the out-of-pocket amounts to compare the actual costs of each plan.

Provider Visits

	PPO Plan		HDHP/HSA Plan	
2 Annual Preventive Exams	Preventive covered at 100%	$0	Preventive covered at 100%	$0
Emergency Room, Surgery, Labs, and Prescriptions for Bicycle Accident	All expenses above out-of-pocket maximum paid 100% by health plan	$19,735	All expenses above out-of-pocket maximum paid 100% by health plan	$19,735
Out-of-Pocket Maximum	Entire amount paid out-of-pocket	$2,500	$2,043 paid from HSA; $2,957 paid out of pocket	$5,000

Case Study 3: (cont.)

When Lauren compared "Money In" versus "Money Out", she saw that the HSA-qualified HDHP option gave her family significantly more protection against true out-of-pocket expenses.

	PPO Plan		HDHP/HSA Plan	
Money In				
Employer HSA Contributions		$0	$170.25 x 12 months	$2,043
Money Out				
Annual Premiums	$170.75 x 12 months	$2,049	$0 x 12 months	$0
Total Provider Costs		$2,500		$5,000
Money Out Subtotal		$4,549		$5,000
Less the HSA Employer Contribution		$0		$1800
Total Money Out		$4,549		$3,200
Difference Between PPO and HDHP/HSA Money Out				$1,349 savings
HSA Balance Remaining		$0		$0

Lauren found that with this plan design, she was $1,349 better off by choosing the HDHP/HSA plan with a catastrophic scenario, and she would have been even better off if she had made additional pre-tax contributions to her HSA to pay for the added expenses.

CHAPTER 7

What If?

HSAs, Medical Procedures, and Life Events

You may have your HSA for a long time. While you own it, you could experience many life events that affect your eligibility to have an HSA, the amount you can contribute, who your dependents are, what kinds of distributions you can make, and whether you can accept other kinds of health coverage.

This chapter describes the kinds of decisions you will need to make and which actions to take should you face an unanticipated crisis or major life events—changes in employment, emergency and non-emergency medical issues, marriage or divorce, newborn or adopted children, disability, or death.

Medical Procedures

What If I Need Surgery?

Imagine you have just been told you need surgery. If you understand your HSA-qualified HDHP, you can focus on making the best choices for your long-term medical and financial well-being.

Do Your Homework

Spend time researching your condition, the treatment possibilities, and the risks and benefits of treatments. Use the internet, visit a library, and speak with friends and relatives who may have had a similar condition. Many HSA administrators and health plans offer powerful online tools that offer explanations, photographs, and videos of possible treatments.

Get a Second Opinion

Medical experts agree, if you have been told you need surgery, get a second or third opinion as professionals often have different solutions to fix a health problem.

Most conditions can wait until you and your doctors understand your options. If you are facing major surgery, your HSA may be worth its weight in gold. You can use your HSA to get a second opinion from any expert you choose, whether or not that doctor is in your plan's network.

Even if you have not met your annual deductible, understand your plan's requirements concerning surgery. Many plans require you get authorization for non-emergency surgery and some may require a second opinion before authorization is given. Following the rules of your HDHP can cut waste, save money, and allow you to use your HSA funds when you need them most.

Choose Your Doctor and Hospital: The Role of In-Network Providers

The HSA-qualified HDHP gives you the freedom to use either in-network or out-of-network providers. But if you are facing a major medical event, such as surgery, you will want to fully explore the options in your network before proceeding.

Be sure you know whether your plan has separate out-of-pocket limits for in-network and out-of-network care, then decide whether you want to use a doctor or hospital in or out of your plan's network. If your plan has separate limits, you could wind up paying thousands of dollars more for care that is no better than what you would get from a provider in your network. Additionally, in-network providers will typically accept deeper discounts for care provided than out-of-pocket providers. This can also save you money.

If you do not have much money in your HSA, you may initially have to pay with after-tax income. Many hospitals and physicians accept payments over time. You can use future HSA deposits to make these payments, or to reimburse yourself if you pay the expenses with other funds. You will need to balance this benefit against any interest charges that the hospital or physician may add to your outstanding bill. Interest charges are not allowable HSA expenses.

If you are contemplating surgery, remember there will be many people involved in the procedure in addition to your principal surgeon. For example, the anesthesiologist should also be in your plan's network if you want the best benefits your plan offers. This is true if your plan has separate in- and out-of-network benefits.

Ask your doctor how many different specialists will be involved in your surgery and where your doctor has operating privileges. Then call the hospital and the other specialists and find out if they are part of your network. Your health plan also can provide this information by telephone or, usually, online. If the provider is not part of the network, they may be willing to give you a prompt-payment discount or honor your in-network pricing if you ask in advance. The time you take to explore these questions can save you a lot of money.

Authorizations and Referrals

Make sure you know what your plan's requirements are concerning authorizations and referrals. Your plan may impose financial penalties if you do not get required referrals and authorizations, even if your provider is in your network. Penalties will not count toward meeting your out-of-pocket limit for the year. Choosing not to follow the plan's rules can cost you money.

Example

Negotiating Discounts with an Out-of-Network Provider

Heather is a 34-year-old mother of three who has been referred by her primary care physician to a surgeon for elective gallbladder removal due to pain and polyps.

The surgeon Heather has been referred to is not in her health plan's network. She feels comfortable with this surgeon and wants to use him anyway.

The surgeon's office explains that since Heather has an HSA and can pay promptly, they will offer a discounted fee, charging her only $50 more than a provider would charge in her network.

Heather then finds out that her out-of-network surgeon can perform surgery in both the out-of-network surgery center and the in-network hospital in her town.

Heather's surgeon agrees to schedule Heather's surgery at the in-network hospital, because this will save her significant out-of-pocket expenses.

Heather is willing to pay a little extra money in surgeon fees to have the gallbladder removal performed by the surgeon of her choice.

Because she is informed and selective, Heather saves potentially thousands of dollars by having her surgery performed at the in-network hospital.

What If I Have a Medical Emergency?

An emergency is the sudden onset of a condition or an accidental injury requiring immediate medical or surgical care to avoid death or permanent disability.

Know your plan's rules about whom to call or visit in an emergency.

If you are having a life-threatening emergency, call 911 and go to the nearest hospital.

Generally you, or a representative such as a family member, must communicate with your plan within 24 to 48 hours of the onset of an emergency. However, if you are initially taken to an out-of-network facility, you do not have to change hospitals until your condition stabilizes.

As in the case of surgery, however, treatment of an emergency is likely to be expensive, and you should consider using in-network providers once the danger period has passed.

If your situation is not life-threatening, you may want to call the health plan's urgent care line or nursing hotline before seeking care (the number is generally on the back of your health plan card).

An urgent condition is one that needs treatment within 24 hours to prevent it from turning into a serious or life-threatening illness. Calling first can be especially important if you are out-of-town, as the urgent care line personnel may be able to direct you to an urgent care center or hospital near you that is part of your plan's network (remember, many plans are national in scope and have in-network providers all over the country).

Using an in-network provider will save you money and stretch your HSA. If you are not sure whether your condition is urgent or an emergency, err on the side of caution, head for the emergency room first, and call later.

Other Life Events

What If I Get Married or Add a Child to My Family?

If you get married, give birth, or adopt a child, your health care coverage needs may change. Under the Health Insurance Portability and Accountability Act (HIPAA), you have the right to ask your plan to cover new family member(s) without waiting until the plan's open enrollment period (see Appendix A for more information on HIPAA).

Enrolling a New Spouse or Baby in Your Plan

Enroll a new family member in your plan as soon as possible. If you are changing from an individual plan to family coverage, your allowable HSA contribution will change on the first day of the first full month, after which you become covered by a family-coverage HDHP, which will allow you to contribute more to your HSA. You may choose to make a pro-rated increase in your contributions for the year, or contribute the family maximum for the year if you believe you will stay in a family plan through the testing period.

Stepchildren

You can usually cover a stepchild in your employer's plan, even if you have not formally adopted the child. The child has to live with you in a parent-child relationship and you have to be responsible for his or her support. Some plans require that you or your current spouse be able to claim the child as a dependent for tax purposes before allowing you to enroll the child in your plan.

As with adding a newborn, adding a stepchild to your plan may allow you to increase your HSA contribution. When determining the best way to cover a stepchild, consider the options under your plan, as well as those available if your spouse/partner has a different health plan.

Example

Conflict with Spouse's Family Coverage May Disqualify the HSA

Phil and Paula each have self-only coverage through their employers. Phil has an HSA-qualified HDHP, while Paula has a traditional plan with a low deductible that does not qualify as an HDHP.

Paula acquires custody of her daughter, Mary, who comes to live with them.

Paula wants to cover Mary under her plan. However, her plan only offers individual and family coverage. If she elects family coverage, Phil will no longer be able to contribute to an HSA, since he will be covered under her plan.

But if Phil's plan offers different options, such as self-plus-child, it may make sense for him to cover Mary under his plan.

What If My Adult Child Becomes Covered Under My Family HDHP?

As if the transition from adolescence to adulthood were not bumpy enough, there can be some rough spots when your child is getting through school or other important transitions.

The health care reform law (PPACA) extends parents' health insurance plan's dependent coverage to children until age 26, regardless of the child's marital status. However, the law does not require parents' insurance to cover dependents (spouse or children) of the adult child (the IRS definitions of dependent for health care coverage purposes are different. Make sure you consult your tax preparer, for additional information).

If your adult child up to age 26 is covered by your family HDHP, but does not qualify as your tax dependent, the adult child can open his/her own HSA as long as he/she meets all other HSA eligibility requirements.

Because your adult child is not your spouse, he/she does not have to split the maximum contribution limit for a family with you. He or she can contribute up to the full maximum family limit—$6,550 in 2014 and $6,450 in 2013. Additionally, your adult child's spouse and tax dependents can use the adult child's HSA for qualified medical expenses.

What If My Adult Child Ages Out of My Plan Coverage?

Once your child turns 26 and transitions off of your plan to his or her own plan, you and your child can begin or continue to contribute to your child's HSA if the child is still covered by an HDHP.

Your child can claim the HSA contribution you make to his/her account as an above-the-line income tax deduction (one taken when calculating adjusted gross income and available to taxpayers whether or not they itemize deductions).

What If I Have More than One HSA?

If you have more than one HSA, your total yearly contributions to your HSAs combined cannot be more than the IRS-mandated limits of $3,300 for an individual in 2014 ($3,250 in 2013), or $6,550 for a family in 2014 ($6,450 in 2013), plus the $1,000 for eligible individuals 55 and older.

Individuals with Archer MSAs must reduce the amount contributed (including any additional contribution) to the HSA by the amount of any contribution (including employer contributions) for the year.

What If My Spouse Also Has an HDHP and an HSA?

If you and your spouse have self-only HDHPs under separate plans, you can each open an HSA and contribute the 2014 yearly maximum for an individual, $3,300.

If either spouse has family HDHP coverage and the other spouse does not have disqualifying coverage, you are both treated as having family HDHP coverage for annual contribution purposes.

If each spouse has an HSA and family coverage under a separate plan, the yearly HSA contribution limit for 2014 is $6,550. You and your spouse can split the $6,550 equally or in any way you want, provided your total contributions do not exceed $6,550.

Each spouse 55 and older (and not enrolled in Medicare) can contribute an additional $1,000 catch-up contribution, whether enrolled in family or individual HDHPs.

What If I Get Divorced or Become Legally Separated?

Spouses do not jointly own an HSA. Each must qualify to contribute to an HSA. In the event of a divorce or legal separation, the HSA owned by one spouse may be divided or given in part or full to the other spouse by court judgment.

Changing from Family to Single-Only HDHP Coverage

If you made the maximum family contribution to your HSA and kept your family coverage after the divorce or legal separation, you will not run into any issues with excess contributions.

However, if you and your spouse were covered by a family HSA-qualified HDHP and you change to single coverage after your divorce, you may need to adjust your contributions to ensure you do not over-contribute for the year. You may also want to talk to your tax preparer about how to deal with additional taxes and penalties due to possible excess contributions.

Determine If You Made an Excess Contribution

You may have made an excess contribution if you divorce and change your HDHP coverage to a single plan, have contributed more than $3,300 to your HSA during 2014, and you have not used the full-contribution rule—where the entire yearly contribution is made on the first day of the last month of the tax year. For more information, see chapter 4. Excess contributions are considered income and subject to an additional 6% excise tax. Excess employer contributions are also subject to income tax and excise tax.

You may withdraw some or all of the excess contributions and not pay the excise tax—you are liable for income tax on the amount, if you meet the following conditions:

- You withdraw the excess contributions by the due date of your tax return for the tax year during which the contributions were made.
- You withdraw any interest income earned on the withdrawn contributions and include the earnings as other income on your tax return for the tax year you withdraw the contributions and earnings.

Contributing the Maximum Family Amount Under the Full-Contribution Rule

If you made a maximum yearly contribution for a family under the full-contribution rule, divorced mid-year, and changed your coverage to single under your health plan's HDHP, you will have failed the testing period for eligibility under family coverage. You will have to include the excess contribution amount in your gross income for the current tax year and pay a 20% penalty on the amount.

Example

Making the Maximum Family Contribution Under the Full-Contribution Rule, Then Changing to Single Coverage During the Testing Period

Janetta, 41, enrolled with family coverage in her HDHP on October 1, 2013. Her husband, Jacob is a freelance cabinet maker and does not have his own insurance, so Janetta put him on her plan. They have no children.

Although she enrolled in her HDHP late in the plan year, she was HSA-eligible on December 1, 2013 and was eligible to make the maximum family contribution of $6,550 under the full-contribution rule.

Janetta and Jacob divorced in September 2014. In the divorce settlement, Janetta kept her HSA and changed to single-only coverage in her HDHP. Although she fulfilled the testing period by remaining in her HDHP, she did not fulfill the testing period for family coverage.

Janetta was still eligible for the maximum contribution for a single person under the full-contribution rule.

She subtracted the maximum contribution for single-only coverage ($3,300) from the $6,550 family contribution to determine the amount she overcontributed in 2013.
$6,550 - $3,300 = $3,250

On her 2014 tax return, Janetta added the excess $3,250 to her adjusted gross income and paid an additional 10% tax on that amount.

In January 2014, Janetta made a lump sum contribution of $6,550 thinking she would have family coverage all year. She wanted to have the money earn interest as quickly as possible.

Because she was still eligible for family coverage on September 1, 2014, she was eligible for nine months of family contributions.

She divided $6,550 and $3,300 by 12 to get the prorated monthly contribution for family and single-only coverage.
Family prorated monthly contribution: $6,550 / 12 = $545.83
Single-only prorated monthly contribution: $3,300 / 12 = $275.00

She multiplied the family monthly contribution by nine to get the amount of family-level contribution she was eligible for during 2014. Then she did the same for the single-level contribution for the three months after her divorce.
$545.83 x 9 = $4,912.47
$275.00 x 3 = $825.00

She added the two amounts to get her maximum allowable contribution for the year.
$4,912.47+ $825.00 = $5,737.47

Then she subtracted the amount from the $6,550 she had contributed to find out her excess contribution for 2014.
$6,550 - $5,737.47 = $812.53

Janetta added the $812.53 to her adjusted gross income on her 2014 return, and paid the 6% excise tax for the excess contribution (the penalty was 6% instead of 10%, because she did not make the overcontribution under the full-contribution rule).

COBRA Coverage for the Divorced Spouse

If you and your spouse are both covered under a family plan through one of your employers and divorce, the spouse who is not employed by the plan's sponsor may be entitled to buy COBRA continuation coverage under the plan (for more information on COBRA, see Appendix A).

Divorce is a qualifying COBRA event. Those eligible may be required to pay up to 102% of the employer's cost of coverage for COBRA, and are entitled to coverage for a limited period of time (from 18 months to 36 months), depending on the qualifying event.

The eligibility period may, in some cases, be extended, if another qualifying event occurs during the period of COBRA eligibility.

While the HDHP is subject to COBRA coverage, the HSA is not.

What If I Lose My Job or My Hours Are Reduced?

If you lose your job, change jobs, have your working hours reduced, or your employer changes the plan it offers, you may no longer be covered by an HDHP, and you may lose your eligibility to contribute to an HSA.

Losing your eligibility to contribute to an HSA does not mean you cannot use the HSA. You can still use any balance in the HSA for qualified medical expenses. You continue to own the account as is, even though you can no longer make contributions to it. If you become covered by a qualifying HDHP again in the future, you can resume contributions.

Using Your HSA to Pay COBRA Premiums

COBRA is an important safety net when you lose your employer-sponsored medical coverage. Although the premiums can appear expensive, COBRA coverage protects you in several ways:

- Your qualified medical expenses continue to be covered.
- You are credited for payments toward your deductible made during the current year.
- By maintaining continuous coverage under a health plan, you make it easier to get coverage for pre-existing conditions when you join another health plan later.

A number of job changes can trigger COBRA eligibility, including quitting your job, getting laid off, retiring, or getting fired other than for gross misconduct (gross misconduct is not specifically defined in COBRA or in regulations under COBRA and depends on specific facts and circumstances). Generally, it is assumed that being fired for most ordinary reasons, such as excessive absences or generally poor performance, does not amount to gross misconduct.

If part-time employees are not covered under your plan, a reduction in hours can also trigger COBRA eligibility. A strike by unionized employees can qualify as a change in hours.

If you elect COBRA benefits, you can use your HSA to pay COBRA premiums and can continue to contribute to your HSA.

What If My Spouse Loses His or Her Own Insurance Coverage?

Having a baby is not the only reason you may need to change from self-only to family coverage.

If you have self-only coverage and your spouse loses coverage, you can generally change to family coverage without waiting for your open enrollment period. As in the case of a new child, your allowable HSA contribution also changes on the first day of the month during which you become covered by an HDHP.

What If I Get a New Job?

It is not uncommon for plans to impose a waiting period before newly hired employees can enroll. If you have a new job that imposes a waiting period and have either a self-only HSA-qualified HDHP or COBRA coverage from your last job, you can continue to make HSA contributions during this waiting period. You can also use your HSA funds to pay your COBRA premiums.

If Your New Employer Does Not Have a Waiting Period

If your new employer has an HSA-qualified HDHP, look into rolling your old HSA over to the new one. You are allowed one rollover per year, though you can make an unlimited number of direct trustee-to-trustee transfers.

Know Your State and Local Laws

COBRA is a federal law applicable to employers with at least 20 employees. Your state, county, or city may also have a similar law that has broader coverage, covers even smaller firms, or offers more generous coverage. If the state or local law is more generous than COBRA, the state or local law is the one that applies.

What If My Employer's Company Closes or Files for Bankruptcy?

If your company closes or files for bankruptcy, it may no longer have a health plan, and COBRA coverage will be unavailable.

If, however, another plan is offered through a successor employer, you may have COBRA rights through that employer. If you are offered COBRA coverage, you may use your HSA to pay your premiums.

If no COBRA coverage is available, you can use your HSA to pay for medical expenses or other coverage, including insurance premiums you might be able to buy while receiving unemployment compensation.

What If My Plant or Branch Office Is Closed?

If your plant or branch office is closed but the rest of the company or a parent company remains in business, you must be offered COBRA coverage through your employer. You can use your HSA to pay those premiums.

What If My Company Is Sold and I Lose My Job?

If your company is sold and you lose your job, the buyer may be obliged to provide you with COBRA coverage. If COBRA coverage is available, you can use your HSA to pay those premiums.

What If My Employer Drops My Plan But Stays in Business?

Termination of a health plan does not trigger COBRA eligibility. You can no longer contribute to an HSA if your HDHP is terminated, but you can use your HSA for medical expenses. You can also opt for a traditional low-deductible health plan if offered by your employer. However, if you choose a traditional low-deductible health plan, you cannot contribute to your HSA.

What If I Retire Before I am Eligible for Medicare?

Many people retire before 65, the age for Medicare eligibility.

If you retire before 65, you can use your HSA for a wide range of medical expenses. You can use it to pay COBRA premiums, premiums for long-term care insurance, or non-COBRA premiums for coverage you may buy on your own (if you are receiving unemployment compensation). You may also use your HSA balance to directly pay for qualified medical expenses.

If you retire from your job, accept a pension from your employer, and go to work for another employer, you cannot use your HSA to make premium payments your new employer may require, unless you are at least 65.

What If I Enroll in Medicare?

Once you enroll in Medicare, you are no longer eligible to make HSA contributions. Remember, enrolling in SSI (the income portion of Social Security) automatically enrolls you in Medicare Part A.

Like the early retiree, you can use the HSA once you have reached 65 to pay COBRA premiums, premiums for long-term care insurance, or non-COBRA premiums for coverage you buy on your own (if you are receiving unemployment compensation). You can also use your HSA balance to pay qualified medical expenses directly.

If you remain employed after 65, you can use your HSA to pay your share, if any, for employer-sponsored health care coverage.

If your employer offers health care coverage to retirees or their survivors and requires a premium contribution from participating retirees or survivors, your HSA can be used to pay for that coverage as well.

You can also use your HSA to pay Medicare premiums once you reach 65.

Medicare recipients should realize that Medigap insurance—a private insurance that covers out-of-pocket costs not covered by Medicare—is not a qualified expense that can be paid with your HSA. Medigap is not the same thing as retiree health insurance; you buy a Medigap policy from a private insurer, while your employer provides retiree health insurance. If you have retiree health insurance, you will generally not need Medigap coverage.

What If I Declare Bankruptcy or Have Other Financial Problems?

An HSA is not protected from creditors unless it qualifies as an employer-sponsored benefit plan under the Employee Retirement Income Security Act (ERISA) of 1974.

ERISA is the federal law that governs the terms under which employee benefit plans are offered. According to the U.S. Department of Labor, an HSA, whether offered by an employer or opened by an individual, is not necessarily an ERISA plan.

There is no exemption in the law specifically protecting HSA balances from the reach of bankruptcy creditors. This means that if the balance in the HSA is taken and used towards the outstanding debits of other creditors, the account holder is subject to income tax and the 20% penalty on the amount used for nonqualified withdrawals.

However, under the 2005 federal bankruptcy law, an individual debtor may deduct any reasonably necessary health insurance, disability insurance, and health savings account expenses for the debtor, the spouse of the debtor or the dependents of the debtor when determining his or her statement of monthly income.

Can I Use My HSA as Collateral for a Loan or Cash It In to Pay a Debt?

Account beneficiaries (the owner) and HSA trustees and custodians cannot enter into a prohibited transaction with the HSA. A prohibited transaction is the sale, exchange, or lease of property, borrowing or lending money, furnishing goods, services or facilities, transferring to or use by or for the benefit of the beneficiary of any assets contained in the account.

The beneficiary also may not pledge the assets of the HSA. Any amount used for such purposes is treated as a distribution, because it is not used for medical expenses, and included in the beneficiary's gross income. A 20% excise tax penalty for such distributions applies.

What If I Become Disabled?

Since you do not need to work in order to make HSA contributions, you can continue to be covered by your employer's or another HSA-qualified HDHP plan after becoming disabled.

If you are covered by an HSA-qualified HDHP and qualify for short-term or long-term disability benefits under your employer-sponsored plan, nothing should change if your employer's health care coverage remains the same during the disability period.

However, there are important cautions. Your HSA has to be paired with an HDHP, so if you lose HDHP coverage under your employer's plan because you can no longer work, you will no longer be eligible to contribute to an HSA unless you qualify for COBRA or can find a qualifying HDHP as an individual. You can use your HSA balance to make COBRA payments if you become eligible for COBRA coverage.

HSAs and Social Security Disability Insurance

If you qualify for Social Security Disability Insurance (SSDI) benefits, everything changes. Qualifying for SSDI benefits is a separate process from qualifying for benefits under an employer-sponsored disability plan. By law, to qualify for SSDI benefits, you must be unable to do any substantial amount of work* due to your health, your condition must have lasted a year and be expected to last at least a year, or be expected to result in your death.

Applicants have to be unable to do substantial work for at least five months before filing an application. Roughly half of SSDI applications are rejected. If you are awarded SSDI benefits, you become eligible for Medicare coverage two years later.

You can use your HSA both during the application process and after you are awarded benefits. Prior to being awarded SSDI benefits, you can use your HSA to pay COBRA premiums if eligible. You can also use your HSA for other medical expenses.

*According to IRS Publication 524, "Substantial gainful activity is the performance of significant duties over a reasonable period of time while working for pay or profit, or in work generally done for pay or profit. Full-time work (or part-time work done at your employer's convenience) in a competitive work situation for at least the minimum wage conclusively shows that you're able to engage in substantial gainful activity".

What If I Die?

When the account owner dies, any amount remaining in the HSA passes to the entity or individual named as the HSA's beneficiaries. If the owner's surviving spouse is the named beneficiary, the HSA becomes the HSA of the surviving spouse.

An HSA is considered an individual account, and as such, the spouse inheriting the HSA is considered the owner. The spouse can then use the HSA as any other HSA owner would. The surviving spouse is subject to income tax on amounts in the account only if not used for qualified medical expenses.

If the HSA passes to a person or persons other than a surviving spouse, the HSA ceases to be an HSA, and the heir or heirs are required to include the fair market value of the HSA as gross income. Fair market value is calculated as of the date of the account owner's death and is reduced by any payments made from the HSA on behalf of the decedent within one year of death.

Choose a beneficiary when you set up your HSA. What happens to that HSA when you die depends on who you designate as the beneficiary. If your estate is the beneficiary, the value of your HSA is included on your final income tax return.

The amount taxable to a beneficiary other than the estate is reduced by any qualified medical expenses for the decedent that are paid for the decedent by the beneficiary within one year of the date of death.

Spouse Is the Designated Beneficiary

If your spouse is the designated beneficiary of your HSA, your HSA will be treated as your spouse's HSA after your death.

Spouse is not the Designated Beneficiary

If your spouse is not the designated beneficiary of your HSA:

- The account stops being an HSA.
- The fair market value of the HSA becomes taxable to the beneficiary in the year you die.

If your estate is the beneficiary, the value of your HSA is included on your final income tax return. The amount taxable to a beneficiary other than the estate is reduced by any qualified medical expenses for the decedent that are paid for the decedent by the beneficiary within one year of the date of death.

Things to Remember

- Research all options for using your HSA. Familiarize yourself with qualified medical expenses, investment options, and other rules and regulations.

- Qualifying life events—marriage, divorce, a new baby, stepchildren, adoption, changing/losing a job, disability, death—all present new coverage needs. Be sure to make the necessary enrollment changes as soon as the opportunity presents itself.

- In most cases, you must make your enrollment or coverage changes within 30 days of the life event.

- HSAs can help you with employment changes and transitions in and out of the workforce.

- Enrolling in Medicare puts an end to making contributions to your HSA. However, you can still use the funds you have built up in your HSA for a variety of expenses.

CHAPTER 8

Using an HSA with Other Tax-Advantaged Accounts

For more than a decade, employers have offered components of consumer-driven health plans (CDHPs) through savings accounts, such as health reimbursement arrangements (HRAs), flexible spending accounts (FSAs), and state and federal Archer medical savings accounts (MSAs). These accounts are used to pay for medical co-payments, dependent care, dental and vision expenses, and other costs with tax-deductible or pre-tax dollars.

Each kind of account offers its own unique advantages. In some situations, supplementing HSAs with different combinations of special-purpose FSAs and/or HRAs gives an employer useful options for making a CDHP strategy better fit both their needs and the needs of their employees.

FSAs and HRAs can also be effective ways to stretch your HSA balance and maximize money you save or use.

You remain eligible to contribute to an HSA if you have a limited-purpose FSA or HRA, as opposed to traditional general-purpose versions of these accounts.

Post-deductible FSAs and HRAs can also be used with an HSA.

Background

MSAs and Archer MSAs

While MSAs and Archer MSAs have existed since the mid-1990s, this federal pilot program was limited to small employers and the self-employed as an affordable alternative to high-priced, low-deductible health plans. MSAs required the individual to also have an HDHP. Savings in the MSA could be rolled over year to year.

MSAs were superseded by HSAs, and existing MSAs grandfathered. The pilot program for Archer MSAs ended December 31, 2007, and no new Archer MSAs can be opened.

HRAs

HRAs are benefit plans that employers can fund and offer alone or with other health benefits. Employers have complete flexibility to customize their HRA plan design. Unused funds may rollover to a subsequent HRA plan year, depending on the plan design.

Self-employed persons are not eligible to participate in an HRA.

In an HRA, the employer funds an account from which the employee is reimbursed for qualified medical expenses, such as co-payments, deductibles, vision care, prescriptions, and dental expenses. Reimbursements are tax-free for the employee and tax-deductible for the employer.

FSAs

An FSA allows employees to set aside pretax earnings to pay for benefits or expenses that are not covered by insurance or other benefit plans, such as co-pays, deductibles, dental and vision expenses, and childcare expenses.

On October 31, 2013, the IRS issued notice 2013-71 with important IRS updates to FSAs. The law was changed to allow employers to rollover $500 in their employees' FSAs to the following year. Employers must choose between offering employees the option to rollover their FSA dollars to the next year, or to have a grace period option for claims incurred after the end of the year.

Check with your employer to find out which FSA option they offer.

If you are enrolled in a general health care FSA with a grace period and you decide to enroll in an HSA-qualified plan for the following year, you will not be able to contribute to an HSA until your run-out period ends and you have no funds remaining in your general health care FSA.

Your employer may allow you to rollover unused funds in an FSA to the following plan year, even if you do not make an election into an FSA.

Using HSAs With Other Benefit Plan Options

The IRS allows employers to offer HRAs and FSAs with an HSA. HSAs can also be used with employee assistance plans (EAPs) and cafeteria plans.

Having general health care FSAs and HRAs can make you ineligible to contribute to an HSA. However, employers are allowed to offer restricted FSAs and HRAs along with their HSA-qualified HDHPs, as long as the FSAs and HRAs meet certain requirements.

Limited-Purpose FSA (LPFSA) or Limited-Purpose HRA

One way for employers to offer an FSA or HRA to employees covered by an HSA-qualified HDHP is to offer a limited-purpose version of these plans.

A limited-purpose FSA (LPFSA) or a limited-purpose HRA may be restricted to paying for permitted coverage benefits, such as only dental and vision expenses.

Limited-purpose FSAs and HRAs work in parallel with an HSA; both kinds of accounts may be used to pay for expenses at the same time.

One advantage of an LPFSA is that all of the money in the account is available to you at the start of the plan year, even if you have not made all of your contributions to the account.

It probably only makes sense to contribute to an LPFSA if you choose to contribute the entire allowable yearly maximum to your HSA. The main disadvantage is that you must forfeit all unspent FSA funds at year-end or when the run-out or grace periods ends, unless your employer allows you to rollover up to $500.

Example

Maximizing Tax-Advantages Through an LPFSA.

Spencer has an HSA with an LPFSA that covers vision and dental expenses only.

Last year when his wife, Melissa, took their small son to the dentist, they were advised he would need a dental appliance to correct a jaw problem. Melissa asked the dentist for a cost estimate. She also got an estimate for dental work Spencer would need during the coming year.

Melissa also wants to replace her prescription sunglasses. She contacts several optical shops to compare costs and gets estimates for exams, frames, and lenses.

In 2014, Spencer and Melissa want to maximize their HSA, so they can start investing it. Spencer sets up his payroll deductions to contribute the full maximum for a family—$6,550. Then he elects to contribute $2,300 to his FSA (based on the estimates for dental work and glasses).

This equals $8,850 of income Spencer and Melissa are able to protect from taxes.

With the FSA to pay the dental and vision expenses, Spencer and Melissa are able to invest their entire HSA contribution for the year in a mutual fund.

Post-Deductible Health Care FSA or HRA

Alternatively, a general-purpose health care FSA or an HRA can be set up to provide benefits only after the minimum annual deductible specified in the HDHP has been satisfied. This is called a post-deductible FSA or post-deductible HRA.

In this case, the FSA or HRA works in cooperation with the HSA. These arrangements do not pay or reimburse any medical expenses incurred before the IRS minimum annual deductible amount is met. For example, either account may be set up to pay benefits only after the IRS minimum deductible is met. After that, the account covers any remaining co-payments or coinsurance for which you are responsible.

If your employer provides an HSA-qualified HDHP with a post-deductible FSA or HRA, you can submit your receipts for reimbursement only after you meet your IRS minimum deductible.

Example

Covering the Gap Between the Deductible and the HDHP's Out-of-Pocket Maximum

Kelly's employer offers an HDHP with a $3,000 deductible and a $4,000 out-of-pocket maximum.

To help close the gap between the plan's deductible and the out-of-pocket maximum, Kelly's employer also offers a $500 post-deductible HRA.

Kelly has a lot of medical expenses during the year and she spends her entire HSA contribution of $3,300. After meeting her deductible and paying her coinsurance, she submits a reimbursement request to HR and receives $500 from the HRA.

Combining Two Kinds of FSAs and HRAs

An FSA and HRA can each be a combination of both limited-purpose and post-deductible, as long as the employer has it written accordingly in the plan document.

Suspended HRA

Before the beginning of an HRA coverage period, you can elect to suspend an HRA. The HRA does not pay or reimburse the medical expenses incurred during the suspension period, except for preventive care and items listed under other health coverage. When the suspension period ends, you are no longer eligible to make contributions to an HSA.

Retirement HRA

A retirement HRA pays or reimburses only those medical expenses incurred after retirement (and no expenses incurred before retirement). In this case, the individual is an eligible individual for the purpose of making contributions to the HSA before retirement, but loses eligibility for coverage periods when the retirement HRA begins to pay or reimburse section 213(d) medical expenses. Thus, after retirement, the individual can no longer contribute to an HSA.

Employee Assistance Programs (EAPs)

An EAP is an employee benefit that covers all or part of the cost for employees to receive counseling, referrals, and advice in dealing with stressful issues in their lives.

An employee covered by an EAP, wellness program, or a disease management plan can still contribute to an HSA, as long as these plans do not provide substantial medical benefits.

Cafeteria Plans

An employer may offer an HSA as part of a cafeteria plan, an employee benefit plan that allows employees to choose benefits from a number of different options, including 401(k), health insurance, other insurance, and time off. HSA contributions can be made through cafeteria plans.

Many of the rules governing HSAs offered as part of a cafeteria plan are different from those governing HSAs offered outside of such a plan. For example, an employer offering an HSA as part of a cafeteria plan can structure its contributions as matching contributions, which means the employee receives an employer contribution only if the employee also contributes to the account. In such a situation, some employees might not receive any contributions to an HSA or might receive contributions that differ in dollar amounts or as a percentage of the HDHP deductible.

In contrast, an employer offering an HSA that is not part of a cafeteria plan must ensure that all eligible participating employees receive a comparable contribution to their HSA plan—either in dollar terms or as a percentage of the HDHP deductible.

At the same time, employer HSA contributions made under a cafeteria plan must meet nondiscrimination rules applicable to cafeteria plans. These are the same rules applied for 401(k)s and FSAs, to ensure that a plan does not favor the employer's most highly compensated employees.

Paying for a Medical Expense Covered by More than One Account

You cannot be reimbursed for the same medical expense from more than one account or arrangement. However, if you have an HSA, a health care FSA, and an HRA that pay or reimburse the same medical expense, the health care FSA or the HRA may pay or reimburse the medical expense, subject to the ordering rules in Notice 2002-45, Part V. Additionally, you must certify to your employer that the expense has not been reimbursed under the other healthcare account and that you will not seek reimbursement under any other plan or arrangement covering that expense (including the HSA).

Contributing to an HSA During the FSA Grace Period

General-Purpose FSA Grace Period

If you have a general-purpose health care FSA, you may have a grace period of up to two-and-a-half months after the plan year ends—a total of 14½ months—to use balances accumulated in your account during the plan year. Most grace periods let you continue to incur expenses and get reimbursed, while a run-out period lets you only be reimbursed for expenses incurred during the plan year. This extension is not automatic; your employer must amend the plan to make it available.

You are eligible to make HSA contributions during an FSA grace period that spill into the next plan year if either of the following condition is met:

- The balance in the general-purpose health care FSA at the end of the prior plan year is zero.

If you still have funds in the general-purpose FSA during the grace period, you cannot begin contributing to your HSA for the current plan year until the first day of the month following the end of the grace period.

Examples

General-Purpose Health Care FSA with a Balance Carried into the Grace Period

Vernon ended his traditional plan/general health care FSA coverage on December 31, 2013, and began an HSA-qualified HDHP on January 1, 2014. Because he still has money in the FSA at the beginning of the new plan year, he cannot begin contributing to his new HSA until after the FSA's grace period ends on March 15, 2014. Because HSA eligibility always begins on the first day of the month, he must wait until April 1, 2014, to make his first HSA contribution.

General-Purpose Health Care FSA with a Zero Balance

Anita had a traditional health plan and a general health care FSA in 2013. She starts her HDHP and HSA on January 1, 2014. She is still technically covered by her FSA during the grace period until March 15, 2014. However, because she had spent her FSA down to zero by December 31, 2013, she can begin contributing to her HSA on January 1, 2014.

LPFSA Grace Period

You do not lose your eligibility to contribute to an HSA if you have funds in an LPFSA during the FSA grace period.

Example

LPFSA with a Balance Carried into the Grace Period

Lorenzo had an LPFSA that only covered vision and dental during 2013. On January 1, 2014, he begins his new HSA-qualified HDHP coverage.

Although there are still funds in the FSA during the FSA's grace period in the new plan year, there is nothing to stop him from making contributions to his HSA starting on January 1, 2014.

Because his FSA is limited-purpose, it does not make Lorenzo ineligible to contribute to his HSA.

CHAPTER 9

Taxes, Paperwork, and Record Keeping

Why Record Keeping Is Important

The balance in your HSA is your money. Treat it and related records as you would your retirement plan, any other savings account, or a credit card. Make sure you understand the charges to your account and get explanations for any you do not understand or do not think belong to you.

Disputes or questions about billing and payments can arise even a year or two after a procedure or office visit (see further discussion about providers that are slow to bill later in this chapter). To reduce these issues, it is particularly important to keep records that allow you to reconstruct how you have spent your money.

It is also important to have records to back up deductions claimed on your tax return, in case you are audited by the IRS.

Submitting Expenses

Keeping track of HSA expenses, contributions, and earnings is much like sorting expenses you deduct on your income taxes from those you cannot deduct. You have to learn a new paradigm for sorting health expenses by category.

Submitting Expenses to the HDHP

If your provider participates in your plan's network, the provider should submit your claim to your plan. If not, you may have to file the claim yourself, so your expenditure is credited toward your deductible and/or out-of-pocket limit. The plan should supply you with a form for filing claims, but many providers give you enough information on your walk-out statement—what you get as you leave the office—then you can use that statement itself to file your claim. Keep copies of your statement in case of a dispute.

Submitting Expenses to the HSA

You can pay HSA-eligible expenses with a debit card if one is provided by your HSA administrator, or with a checkbook that draws from your HSA. Alternatively, you can pay using your own account or credit card and submit the expense for reimbursement.

Some HSA administrators let account holders electronically transfer funds from the HSA to their own account for reimbursement.

Regardless of how you get reimbursed, you can only be reimbursed for the expenses you incurred after your HSA was established.

Submitting Expenses to an FSA

If you had an FSA in the past and your employer converts an HDHP with a limited purpose FSA (LPFSA), you will not have a lot of new processes or paperwork to learn. You submitted expenses to your old FSA by providing an EOB or a benefit denial from your health plan; an LPFSA is likely to work the same way.

Paperwork You Will Receive

Invoices and Point-of-Sale Receipts

Even though most over-the-counter medications required a doctor's prescription in order to be considered a medical expense as of January 1, 2011, there are still many other items you can purchase with your HSA debit card or checks through retail stores, such as diabetic supplies, canes, reading glasses, and bandages.

The important thing to remember is to be sure all receipts and invoices have as much detail about the goods or services provided or purchased as possible, including date, item, service description, vendor, etc.

Explanation of Benefits (EOB)

The EOB is a summary of charges and payment responsibilities provided by your health plan. It shows how much your health plan paid the provider, how much the provider originally charged, and the contracted discounts to which your providers have agreed.

The EOB also shows your financial responsibility. The EOB summarizes the cost of the services provided during the doctor's visit, and updates both the status of the HSA—if you used your card to pay—and the owner's progress toward meeting the plan deductible.

Note that the EOB also explains the participant's right to dispute any statements made in the EOB.

HSA Statement

Your HSA administrator should send or make available a periodic statement detailing your contributions; those your employer may have made on your behalf, payments made to providers from your HSA, investment and/or interest earnings accrued to your account, and fees your account may have incurred. Keep your statements the same way you do for other financial accounts—maybe in the same place.

Sample of Explanation of Benefits

THIS IS NOT A BILL
(Please keep this form for your records)

EXPLANATION OF BENEFITS (EOB)

John Doe
123 Any Street
Any Town, ST, 90062

Date: **March 12, 2014**
Benefit Plan Number: **XYZ00000000A**
Page Number: **1 of 1**

Participant: **John Doe**
Patient: **John Doe**
Relationship: **Subscriber**

Member Services
Local: **000.000.0000**
National: **800.000.0000**

Payment Summary

Patient/Claim No.	Paid to	Total Charges	Covered Amount	Previously Processed	Patient Responsibility
John D 1234567890		$135.00	$60.00	$0.00	$75.00

Subscriber's Responsibility: $75.00
Does not reflect any payments you may have made to the provider.

Year-to-Date Cost Sharing Status: 2014

Applied to $3,000 per member deductible:
John D. $75.00
$75.00 has accumulated toward deductible maximum.

Sample of Periodic HSA Statement

If you have any questions,
please call **800.000.0000**

John Doe
123 Any Street
Any Town, ST, 90062

Account Statement
Account Number: **123456**
Period: **01/01/2014 to 01/30/2014**
Statement Print Date: **02/01/2014**

Date	Description of Transaction	Deposit or (Withdrawal)	Account Balance
		Beginning Balance	$ 8,803.98
06/02/2014	Employer Contribution for 2014	$83.33	$8,887.31
06/02/2014	Employer Contribution for 2014	$89.58	$8,976.89
06/03/2014	Payment for Claim 219325-0142	($15.00)	$8,961.89
06/15/2014	Employer Contribution for 2014	$89.58	$9,051.47
06/15/2014	Employer Contribution for 2014	$249.99	$9,301.46
06/21/2014	Payment for Claim 219325-0143	($102.74)	$9,198.72
06/30/2014	Payment for Claim 219325-0146	($244.69)	$8,954.03
06/30/2014	Investment: Fund A	($1,043.10)	$7,910.93
06/30/2014	Investment: Fund B	($695.40)	$7,215.53
06/30/2014	Investment: Fund C	($1,043.13)	$6,172.40
06/30/2014	Investment: Fund D	($695.40)	$5,477.00
06/30/2014	Investment: Fund E	($695.40)	$4,781.60
06/30/2014	Investment: Fund F	($695.40)	$4,086.20
06/30/2014	Investment: Fund G	($695.40)	$3,390.80
06/30/2014	Investment: Fund H	($695.40)	$2,695.40
06/30/2014	Investment: Fund I	($695.40)	$2,000.00
06/30/2014	Interest for Jun-10 (Annual percentage yield earned for period is 1.25% on average collected balance of $8,864.03)	$9.18	$2,009.18
		Ending Balance	$ 2,009.18

Investment Portfolio

Fund	Category	Shares	Closing Price	Closing Value
Fund A	Small Cap Fund	73.14	$18.71	$1,368.51
Fund B	Small Cap Stock Index	82.71	$16.34	$1,351.48
Fund C	Blue Chip Value	223.25	$9.10	$2,031.61
Fund D	Emerging Markets	34.82	$41.06	$1,429.71
Fund E	International Market Masters	93.76	$15.12	$1,417.65
Fund F	Appreciation Fund	43.90	$31.39	$1,378.12
Fund G	Capital Appreciation	66.34	$20.72	$1,374.65
Fund H	Equity Income Fund	69.49	$19.52	$1,356.46
Fund I	Large Cap Index	108.47	$18.89	$2,048.92
			Ending Balance	$13,757.11

You Can Spend Your HSA Over a Considerable Amount of Time

Because an HSA is intended to serve, at least in part, as a long-term savings vehicle, you can accumulate funds over a considerable period of time. There is no time limit for claiming a reimbursement from your account, as long as you incur the expense you are claiming after the HSA was established. That may mean you need to produce or recover records about contributions to the account, long after a transaction occured (for example, what was paid out of the account, and when and why the transaction was made).

A Provider Who Is Slow to Bill Can Complicate Your Life

Some busy hospitals or medical practices can lose your claim or bill. There have been cases where the doctor's office filed the claim online and it came through illegibly, so the office filed it again and it came through illegibly, again. Or maybe the hospital or doctor's office changed billing systems and some claims were lost in the transition. End result: the bill goes unsubmitted for payment for many months.

Any plan is responsible for covered expenses you incur while a member of that plan, but once the plan is closed, their responsibility expires.

Your former plan has to keep a reserve so claims participants can submit expenses after the plan is closed. However, this reserve may not be very large and can get exhausted before a late claim is considered.

That is not necessarily the slow-billing provider's problem. When you went in for your visit or procedure, you signed a paper saying you would pay if your plan did not.

Always alert providers if you are changing insurance plans or have been advised that your employer is planning to do so. Encourage providers to submit any outstanding bills promptly.

Keeping Track of Deductibles

The EOB you receive from your HDHP will show your progress toward meeting the plan limits for the year. Make sure you know how to interpret the deductible information in the EOB and always try to work from the most recent statement so you can make the right decisions about your care and how to pay for it.

Different Rules May Apply to In-Network and Out-of-Network Care

Most plans that include provider networks apply different out-of-pocket limits, deductibles, or both, to in-network and out-of-network care. In a traditional plan, this did not matter to you, unless you or your family had a particularly costly year.

In an HSA-qualified HDHP, your deductible may be half or more of your out-of-pocket limit, so you are more likely to hit the out-of-pocket limit than in a traditional plan. This means you may want to keep track of your in-network and out-of-network spending and adjust your provider choices if you are close to meeting one limit but not the other.

Example

Selecting a Network Provider

Suppose Roy has a self-only plan with a $1,700 out-of-pocket limit for in-network care and a $2,600 limit for out-of-network care.

In-network care is insured at 100%; out-of-network care at 80%. His plan's deductible is $1,700.

Roy has spent $1,600 so far this year for in-network care and $250 for out-of-network care. He is considering foot surgery that will cost $2,000.

He can choose an in-network provider or one out of his network. If he chooses an in-network provider, he will pay $100, no matter what price the provider has negotiated with his plan. If he chooses an out-of-network provider, he will pay $400 ($2,000 x 20% non-network coinsurance).

If You Are Not in an Integrated Plan

If you do not have an HSA administrator that integrates with your insurance company and gives you a history of all of the claims paid by your HSA, be especially diligent about tracking your payments.

Always reconcile the paperwork you receive from your HDHP with statements from your HSA. If you have had a problem with your HDHP and/or HSA, you may have to follow up with both your health plan and HSA administrator to make sure errors are corrected in both accounts.

Disputing Charges

If you get a bill that does not make sense, call your provider's office, the customer service number provided for your plan, or both. If someone sent you an incorrect statement, it can become a problem later, unless you do something about it.

Everybody makes mistakes and a busy medical practice, in particular, will be dealing with a large number of plans that may be constantly changing requirements, and patients whose plans are changing as well. Keep track and follow up.

When You Disagree with Your HDHP

Some of the same claims-processing errors possible under a standard insurance plan can also happen under an HSA-qualified HDHP. An in-network provider's invoice might be incorrectly processed as out-of-network, or the birth date for a participant could be incorrectly recorded, resulting in a denial of benefits.

Because your progress toward meeting the year's deductible can be affected, it is recommended that you immediately follow up on errors.

When You Disagree with Your HSA Statement

If you have never had an unauthorized charge appear on a credit card, you are part of an elite club. You do not have to be a victim of identity theft—a simple processing error can put a charge on your account that belongs to someone else.

If your HSA issues you a debit or credit-type card, check charges on your HSA just as you do the charges on your credit card statements. Understand your rights to have a disputed charge investigated and/or removed. If your HSA issues your checks, understand your rights to stop payment on a check, and what to do if you lose your checkbook.

You are Responsible for Documenting How You Used Your HSA

In a traditional plan, your plan pays for only what it covers. Typically, the covered services are outlined in the plan documents you get from your insurer or the summary plan description (SPD) you get from your employer.

The HSA, in contrast, can be used for a wide range of expenses limited only by HSA legislation and generally what is accepted by the IRS for itemized medical deductions.

You need to understand what the allowable uses are and back up your claims with receipts. If you do not, you may face a 20% penalty plus taxes for unauthorized distributions. If you spend the money on items other than eligible medical expenses before you turn 65, you will also be required to pay income taxes on the expense.

Keep Your Original Documents

Any home financial software or spreadsheet program can be used to help you budget and keep track of medical expenses. However, if you need to substantiate or contest a claim, you will need the original documents. Some HSA administrators provide mobile apps to photograph and store these documents.

Keeping Good Records Helps Avoid Confusion

Your HSA and your HDHP can be used for different types of health care expenses. Make sure you know what each plan covers, and that each covers what it should.

Keep your HSA records as long as the account remains open, even if you have moved your account to a different bank or other company from the one where you first established your account, and you are no longer eligible to contribute to your account.

The Importance of the Calendar

There are several reasons why it is important to keep track of when expenses occurred and were paid.

Coordinating Account Management with the IRS Calendar

The HSA is a tax-favored account, so the IRS has something to say about how you spend your balance. You can wait as long as you want after the expense has been incurred to submit it to your HSA (find more information later in this chapter on how long to keep HSA records). However, no matter how old the expense is, you must be prepared to fully document it in the year you claim it.

Coordinating Account Management with the HDHP Calendar

The HSA is yours, but the HDHP may only be yours for now. Your employer may change from an HDHP offered by one company to one offered by another, or may eliminate your HDHP entirely in favor of another plan design.

If your current HDHP is replaced by another, be sure any expenses you accrue are paid by the correct plan and coordinate your HSA with the new HDHP. If your employer changes plans and you can no longer be covered by an HDHP, you need to keep track of when this happens, as you will no longer be able to contribute to your HSA as of the first day of the first month after the month your HDHP coverage ends. For example, if your HDHP coverage ends on June 15, you are no longer eligible to contribute to your HSA as of July 1. However, you can continue to use the funds in your HSA for eligible expenses.

How Long to Keep Receipts, Statements, and Other Documentation

You are responsible for documenting that your HSA distributions were made for qualified purposes. The HSA custodian or trustee, your insurer, and your employer are responsible for various aspects of your account reporting, but not for this.

The IRS can generally audit most individual taxpayers for three years after the extended due date of the return. This means if your income tax return for 2013 is due April 15, 2014, but you file for the automatic extension to August 15, the IRS can audit you until August 15, 2017.

For some individual taxpayers, that period is five years. For example, if you have a hobby business, your 2013 return can be audited until Aug. 15, 2019. But if the IRS alleges or suspects fraud, they can audit all your returns as far back as they want.

It is suggested that you keep records documenting your HSA distributions for at least the period of time your income tax return is considered "open," or subject to audit, and preferably for as long as you maintain the account.

Avoiding "The Shoebox Effect"

Even if your HSA provider gives you a debit, credit card, or a checkbook, you may end up submitting claims yourself because you forgot to use the HSA, or because when you first established your HSA, you may not have had enough in it to pay claims.

If you stuff your receipts in a shoebox intending to get to them later, you may miss out on important benefits from your account, and you may end up using post-tax dollars when HSA funds were available.

Establish a clearly labeled file and keep track of what you have already submitted, what has been paid, and what is still outstanding. If your health plan offers online access to EOBs, get in the habit of using your plan web site as a ready-made filing system.

HSA and HDHP Records Made Easy

A Simple System for Keeping Track of Your HSA and HDHP Records

Use a simple multipocket folder available in any stationery supply store, a three-ring binder with separators, or scan documents. Financial reports provided by your HSA administrator or by household budget programs, such as Quicken, can also help you track your expenses. Original documents and receipts will be required in the event of an IRS audit. After you have picked your system, set up the following sections:

- **Bills and proofs of payment for care obtained from in-network providers.** Include canceled checks or credit card receipts for any bills you did not pay directly from your HSA.

- **Bills and proofs of payment for care obtained from out-of-network providers.** Again, include canceled checks or credit card receipts for any bills you did not pay directly from your HSA.

- **EOBs from network providers, arranged in reverse chronological order (most recent on top), so you can easily track your progress toward meeting HDHP limits that may apply to your network care.**

- **EOBs from out-of-network providers, again arranged in reverse chronological order, so you can easily track your progress toward meeting any separate HDHP limits that may apply to out-of-network care.** You may not need separate files for in-network and out-of-network care if your HDHP doesn't apply separate limits.

- **Bills and proofs of payment for health care spending that are not covered under your plan, and so not counted toward your deductible.** Such spending could include the excess cost of Braille reading material for a blind person or transportation costs to see a specialist in another city.

- **Periodic statements from your HSA trustee or custodian.** For ease of reference, you may want to arrange this part of your file in reverse chronological order as well, so the first statement you see is the most current.

Label your file with the current year, and set up a new file every year. This will make it easier to track bills and reimbursements as time goes on.

Eligibility for Tax Deductions

The employer, employee, or individual, depending on who makes the contribution, may claim deductions for HSA contributions. HSAs qualify as a deduction for federal and most state taxes.

Deducting Contributions from Others

Although parties other than the account holder or their employer can make contributions to the account holder's HSA, those third parties cannot deduct the contribution from their taxes.

However, the account holder who received the contribution can deduct the contribution from his or her gross income.

Example

Contributing to an Adult Child's HSA

Ernesto and Maria's son Carlos is 25 and still in college.

Carlos is too old to qualify as a tax dependent, but young enough to be covered by his father's HDHP.

Ernesto helps Carlos open his own HSA and makes a $1,000 contribution to the HSA.

Ernesto and Maria cannot deduct the $1,000 on their own tax return, but Carlos can exclude it from gross income on his.

Income Tax Deductions for the Employee or Individual Purchaser

The tax-deductible contribution amount is calculated on a month-to-month basis, based on the total amount of the deduction and the number of months of participation.

The contribution is an above-the-line deduction for the purpose of calculating adjusted gross income, unless done through a cafeteria plan.

Example

Choosing to Use the HSA Contribution as an Above-the-Line Deduction

Hank, a single taxpayer, makes $36,000 a year and contributes $1,000 to his HSA.

On his tax return, he can only deduct medical expenses that exceed 7.5% of his adjusted gross income.

Hank has not had any medical expenses for the year. He decides that it is better to take an above-the-line deduction by subtracting the $1,000 HSA contribution when calculating his adjusted gross income.

Double-Dipping is not Allowed

You *cannot* count an HSA contribution twice by calculating it against your gross income and then deducting it as an itemized medical expense. In fact, no expense can be deducted twice or paid twice from different tax-exempt accounts or through different insurance plans.

As an eligible individual, you can, however, deduct a contribution on your tax return even if another person makes it on your behalf.

Employer-Provided Coverage

Contributions an employer makes to the employee's HSA are treated as employer-provided coverage for medical expenses under an accident or health plan and are excludable from the employee's gross income if made on behalf of an eligible individual.

The employer contributions are not subject to income tax withholding from wages or subject to the Federal Insurance Contributions Act (FICA), the Federal Unemployment Tax Act (FUTA), or the Railroad Retirement Tax Act.

Employer contributions may be subject to certain state taxes.

Contributions for the Self-Employed and Owners of S Corporations

Self-employed individuals and owners of S corporations are not considered employees. As such, they cannot receive employer contributions. However, they can make their own contributions and claim the above-the-line deduction on their personal income tax return.

Contributions to the HSA made by a bona fide partner are treated as a distributive share of partnership income and are considered guaranteed payments derived from the partnership's trade or business and reported as such on IRS Schedule–K1 (Form 1065). The contributions are included in the partner's net earnings, from which the partner is then able to deduct those contributions as an adjustment to gross income, just as any HSA owner is able to do, within the confines of the law.

Contributions to the HSA of a >2% shareholder-employee in consideration for services rendered are treated as a guaranteed payment, and are includable in the >2% shareholder-employee's net earnings. The contributions can then be deducted as an adjustment to gross income.

Tax Deductions for the Employer

To be tax-deductible, employer HSA contributions must be comparable for all employees. There is one exception to this rule. Employers may contribute more to HSAs for non-highly compensated employees. The IRS uses the same definition of highly compensated employees for HSAs as they do for other retirement accounts.

Contributions are considered comparable if the employer makes the same contributions on behalf of all eligible participating employees with comparable coverage during the same period. Contributions are considered comparable if they are either the same dollar amount or the same percentage of the deductible under the HDHP.

For example, Company A's contribution is considered comparable for all employees if each eligible employee gets $500 toward an HSA. Company B's contribution is also considered comparable for all employees if it covers 75% of the deductible.

Even in the case of a husband and wife working for the same employer, the HSAs must be separate as well as the contributions, or comparability rules may be breached because it could be seen that one individual was receiving twice the contribution rather than half of a joint contribution.

Except under cafeteria plans, an employer may not institute matching contributions to HSAs. Comparability rules do not apply when contributions are made through cafeteria plans, however, discrimination testing rules do apply.

IRS-Compliant Paperwork

Form W-2

Wage and Tax Statement

Employers must generally file a Form W-2 for any employee they paid wages and employees must enclose a copy of this form with federal, state, and local income tax returns. Your employer must report employer contributions (which include pretax cafeteria plan deductions to income) to your HSA in Box 12 on your Form W-2.

Form 1040

US Individual Income Tax Return

Your Form 1040 contains a line where you can enter your posttax HSA contribution to calculate your adjusted gross income. You must include any distributions that were not made for qualified medical expenses whether to you, your spouse, or dependents as part of your adjusted gross income. You will be assessed a 20% penalty and be required to pay income taxes on non-qualified distributions.

Form 1099-SA

Distributions from an HSA, Archer MSA, Medicare+ Choice MSA, or Medicare Advantage MSA

Your HSA custodian or trustee will report any HSA distributions to you and to the IRS on Form 1099-SA, which is why you need to be prepared to justify your spending as allowable under the law.

Form 5329

Additional Taxes on Qualified Plans (Including IRAs) and Other Tax-Favored Accounts

Filling out this form will help you determine if you made any contributions or distributions that might be outside the allowable limits for your HSA. If you have had a life event, such as a divorce, this form is a good worksheet for calculating whether your change in coverage caused any additional tax liabilities.

If completion of this form shows that you owe any tax or penalties on non-qualified distributions or excess contributions, you must file this form with your income tax return.

Form 5498-SA

HSA, Archer MSA, Medicare+ Choice MSA, or Medicare Advantage MSA Information

Your HSA trustee or custodian must report contributions to the HSA to the IRS and to you on this form. Any amounts reported on Forms 1099-SA or 5498-SA should agree with what you report on your Form 1040.

Form 8889

HSAs

You must file Form 8889 with your Form 1040 or Form 1040NR if you (or your spouse, if married and file a joint return), had any activity in your HSA during the year. You must file the form even if only your employer or your spouse's employer made contributions to the HSA.

If, during the tax year, you are the beneficiary of two or more HSAs, or you are a beneficiary of an HSA and you have your own HSA, you must complete a separate Form 8889 for each HSA. Enter "statement" at the top of each Form 8889 and complete the form as instructed. Next, complete a controlling Form 8889 combining the amounts shown on each of the statement Forms 8889. Attach the statements to your tax return after the controlling Form 8889.

CHAPTER 10

Guidelines for Employers

Why Are Insurance Rates Increasing So Rapidly?

Most employers who do not have the majority of their employees in HSA-type plans continue to see significant insurance rate premium increases. In contrast, employers that have HSAs in place for their employees tend to see lower rate increases. Effective January 1, 2014, health reform or PPACA will present a number of new requirements and opportunities to employers seeking to offer health related benefits to their employees.

Health Care Costs Are Escalating for Many Reasons

- New technologies and treatments that increase life expectancy
- Rising numbers of patients with chronic illnesses
- Patients' failure to seek lower-cost options (such as generic drugs that may be as effective as brand-name medicines)
- Overutilization of health care facilities (such as emergency rooms for minor illnesses)
- Administrative waste
- State and federal government mandates for extended coverage

Some of the drivers for health care costs are out of employers' control. However, other factors, such as influencing health care utilization patterns, preventing chronic disease through wellness programs, and lowering the average cost of claims offer possibilities for flattening the trend of rising insurance rates by rewarding positive employee behavior.

Poor Visibility of Costs

In many ways, our health care system does not make a direct connection between receiving a service and paying for it. Instead, a third party—the insurance company, employer, or plan administrator—actually processes and pays the bill. The consumer seldom pays attention to the actual price tag.

The consumer is usually only impacted by the amount of his or her co-payment, rather than the full price for office visits, lab tests, etc. The consumer sees the co-payment as the price.

But as services become more expensive, the consumer pays for the increase indirectly through higher premium deductions from wages. The result is that premium costs are putting health care out of reach for employers and individuals.

How Can an HSA Improve the Situation?

An HSA-qualified HDHP can bring both consumer choice and flexibility back into health care by putting more watchdogs in the market to compare costs and demand better value.

Adding the ability to save on taxes and keep some of the savings achieved by careful consumerism provides even more incentive for consumers to take an active role in controlling health care costs.

A Win/Win for Employers and Employees

An HSA program gives employers an opportunity to empower employees to take control of the way they consume health care services. This can, in turn, lower the average cost of claims through better utilization of health care services and help lower your premium costs. It also contributes to significant savings in payroll taxes.

Many employers use the savings achieved through HSA strategies to fund additional benefit offerings for their employees or to retain staff they might otherwise have to downsize. Others choose to use the savings to fund new projects to keep their companies competitive.

The Key to HSA Success

Employers receive the most significant benefits from their HSA strategy once HSA adoption exceeds 50% among the eligible employee population. At that point, the behavior change that affects utilization patterns and average cost of claims reaches critical mass and employers find they have more bargaining power to ask for lower rates from their insurance carriers. Rate trend savings are augmented by additional savings in payroll taxes.

Gradual Migration or Full Replacement?

Some employers choose to offer their employees a single choice in plans—an HDHP with an HSA. This full-replacement strategy escalates the achievement of HSA program objectives.

Other employers, concerned about possible employee backlash or loss of ability to attract top employee talent, choose a more gradual approach by offering multiple benefit plan choices that include an HSA-qualified HDHP option. They usually set an objective of full replacement within three to five years.

Many employers report that they have two primary motivators for adopting the full-replacement approach:

- Their premiums are increasing so quickly, they know they will soon have to start cutting benefits to keep costs low. They have no choice. The traditional low premium/low out-of-pocket plans are becoming unsustainable.

- When they see potential savings modeled in cost projection tools, they conclude that earlier adoption launches a positive chain reaction. High HSA adoption rate ➔ lower premiums ➔ flatter trend ➔ more funds available for making contributions to employees' HSAs ➔ even higher HSA adoption, and so on.

Calculating Projected Savings

In the following example, a company with 1,500 employees has an HSA adoption rate of 8% its first year. Its starting trend is 9%. The company gradually increases employee HSA adoption to 86% over five years. With the savings in taxes and insurance premiums, it is able to save **$8,694,730** net of HSA contributions by the fifth year.

HSA Cost Trend

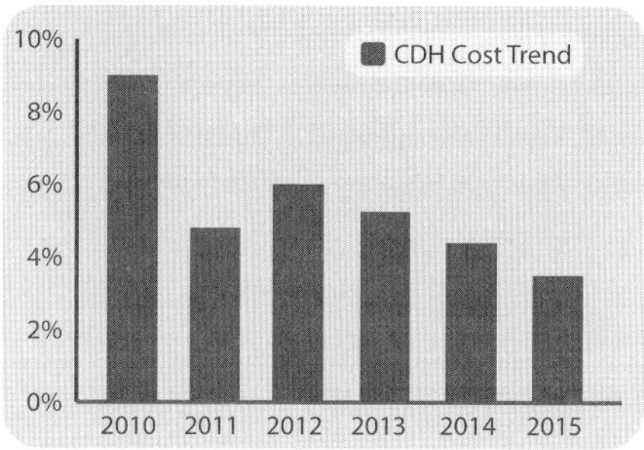

Annual Savings

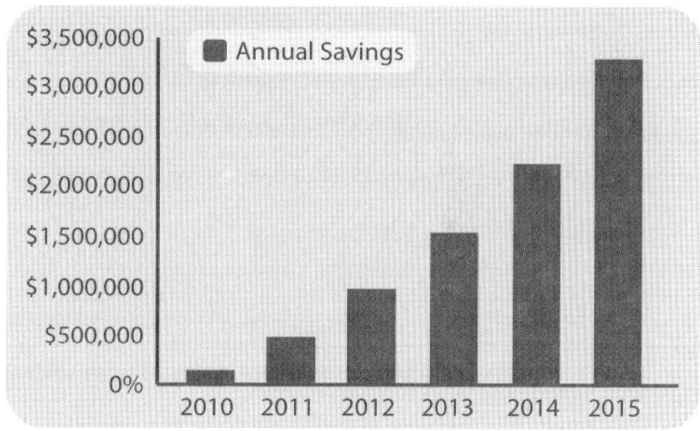

By adopting a full-replacement strategy and starting with 74% adoption the first year of its HSA program, its projected savings over the five-year period increases to **$22,666,633**.

HSA Trend Cost

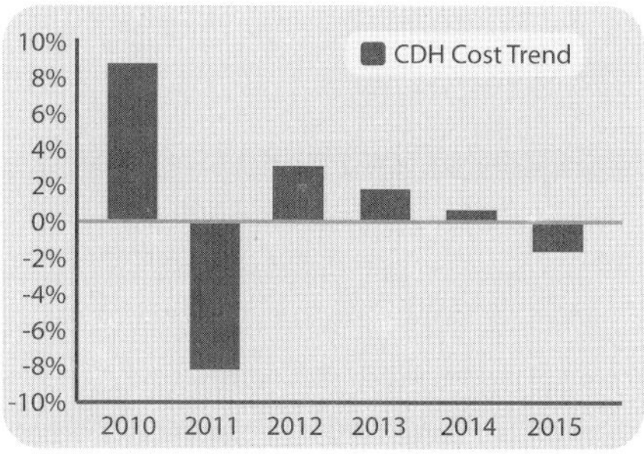

Annual Savings

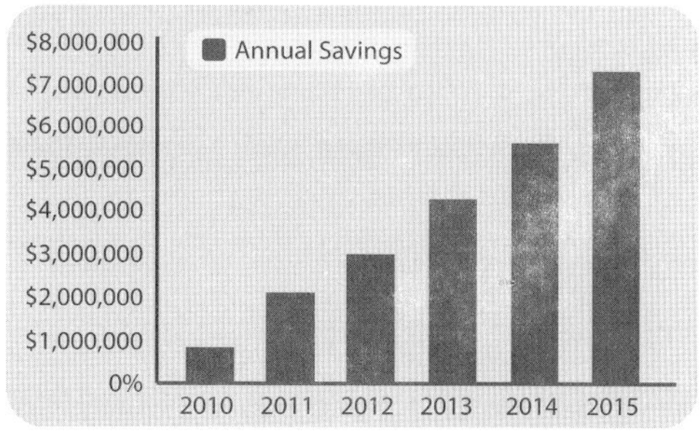

The faster full adoption can be realized, the sooner the HSA strategy can build savings for the employer and healthy HSA balances for employees—letting success build on success to meet full HSA program objectives.

Increasing Adoption

Research is clarifying ways employers can hold down the rising insurance premium trend while shifting some of the premium cost savings to employees' HSAs. The sooner they adopt these ways, the more savings they achieve, and the more benefits they can preserve for employees.

Confronting Perceived Risk

HealthEquity, Inc., the nation's oldest and largest HSA trustee, has conducted research among its client base and concluded there are three main factors that influence an employee's decision whether or not to enroll in an HSA-qualified HDHP.

- **Personal and family health status**
  There is concern about the risk of having major health care expenses before the HSA has enough funds to cover the deductible.

- **Age (implying better health at a younger age)**
  There is a perception that HSA-qualified HDHPs are ideal only for younger, relatively healthy people.

- **Perceived relative financial value of the HDHP vs. the traditional plan**
  Employees are skeptical about their ability to build and keep a large enough balance to achieve significant financial benefit.

There is one overriding account holder concern—risk of exposure to high out-of-pocket costs. Balanced against the perceived safety of a traditional low-deductible health plan, it can be difficult to encourage adoption quickly enough to build traction under a HSA strategy.

Ways to Increase Adoption

Most of the ways to increase adoption that HealthEquity recommends confront the perceived risks through a combination of plan design, communication, and focused enrollment processes.

The following chart shows the various steps a company can take to increase HSA adoption and the relative effectiveness of those steps:

HealthEquity HSA Adoption Best Practices

1. Plan Options

The single-most effective way to encourage adoption is a full-replacement approach that offers only one plan option—the HSA-qualified HDHP. This must be coupled with effective communication and financial incentives to build trust among employees.

HealthEquity's clients who have chosen to offer the full-replacement plan option report that a by-product of the approach is increased social networking among employees to comment on the plan and educate each other. On the other hand, client groups that have chosen the opposite approach, offering three or more plan options, report that their employees consistently remain with the same plans. HSA adoption among those groups remains at 5% or less.

High Adoption	Full-replacement
Med Adoption	Dual option
Low Adoption	3+ options

2. Employee Premium Differentials

When the premium of the HSA-qualified HDHP option is at least 40% less than other plan options, HSA adoption increases significantly.

High Adoption	40%+ differential
Med Adoption	15%–39% differential
Low Adoption	<15% differential

3. Deductible Level

One of the most effective ways to reduce the perception of risk is to keep the deductible as low as possible for the qualified HDHP. HealthEquity has observed that the majority of clients who have achieved high adoption (>30%) set the deductible of the HDHPs to less than 2,000/4,000. They have coupled this with the lowest possible out-of-pocket maximum.

High Adoption	Federally mandated minimum
Med Adoption	Up to \$2,000/\$4,000 single/family
Low Adoption	More than \$2,000/\$4,000 single/family

4. Out-of-Pocket Maximum Level

Another way to reduce risk for employees is to set the out-of-pocket maximum level for the HSA-qualified HDHP option to be equal to that of the other plans offered to employees. Taking that risk away, then offering an employer contribution to the HSA, has improved adoption rates even when two or more alternative plans are offered to employees during open enrollment.

High Adoption	Equal alternative plan(s)
Med Adoption	Up to 50% higher than alternative plan(s)
Low Adoption	51%+ higher than alternative plan(s)

5. HSA Employer Contribution	
Making a meaningful employer contribution to the employees' HSAs reinforces the win/win message of sharing the cost savings from a HSA plan. This has the greatest impact on HSA adoption. The employer contribution also calls attention to the wealth-building aspect of an HSA-qualified HDHP and is a catalyst for social networking. Employees educate each other by discussing ways to build their balances and control costs. It is also an important factor in reducing the perception of risk.	
High Adoption	60%+ of deductible
Med Adoption	25%–59% of deductible
Low Adoption	<25% of deductible

6. Open Enrollment	
It is important to make it easy for employees to choose the HSA-qualified HDHP. Enrollment tools should be easy-to-use and understand. It is more effective to have the HSA-qualified HDHP as the default option if a menu of options is offered.	
High Adoption	Active enrollment with HSA-qualified HDHP as default
Low Adoption	Passive enrollment or active enrollment with non-HDHP default

7. Employee Communication Strategy	
HealthEquity has noted that while all of the most successful client groups had a different mix of ways used to achieve high HSA adoption rates and the resultant cost savings, there was one thing they all had in common: active involvement of company executives in communication campaigns. By starting early, participating in communication activities, and being vocal about their own enrollment in HSA-qualified HDHPs, executives were influential in building enthusiasm for HSA programs. They walked the talk to gain trust.	
High Adoption	Active communication campaign (six months in advance) with executive engagement
Med Adoption	Moderate specified communication campaign (two months in advance)
Low Adoption	No or limited campaign

Way to Achieve Final Success—Employee Education

Education is key to a smooth transition to HSA-qualified health plans. Employees may be uncomfortable with this new type of plan, and many will not understand how it works.

For some who do not understand how the tax savings and premium decreases compare financially to a higher deductible, an HSA-qualified HDHP may look like a reduction in benefits.

In order to help employees get the most benefit from their HSAs, it is important that employers take the proper steps to help employees understand how the new plan works, how to contribute, and how to make payments.

Employers need to help employees assess how much to contribute to an HSA, how to keep records, whom to ask when they have questions, how to check HSA balances, use a network, and get good health care information. The HSA administrator and health plan may have tools to help employers educate employees.

Employers who provide employees with information and tools to help them make better health care decisions, especially decisions on how to use the health care system effectively, will see their employees taking full advantage of the opportunity to increase the equity in their accounts and gain every allowable tax benefit.

Employers and their HSA providers should conduct employee education and communication activities throughout the plan year.

Rules for Employers

A summary of rules that employers should follow to be fully compliant with the laws and regulations governing HSAs follows.

Comparability of Contributions

Employer contributions to employees' HSAs must be comparable for all employees participating in the HSA. Comparability under IRS regulation requires the same dollar amount or the same percentage of the annual deductible amount for the HSA contribution. However, it is only necessary to count employees who are eligible individuals and have the same category of coverage (such as self-only or family). Part-time employees (customarily those who are employed fewer than 30 hours per week) are tested separately. If the employer contributions fail the comparability test, there will be an excise tax imposed on the employer equal to 35% of the amount the employer contributed to the HSA.

Unless it is done through a cafeteria plan, employers may not make matching contributions that are conditioned on a contribution by the employee. For example, through a cafeteria plan, an employer may offer to contribute $500 to your account on the condition that you contribute some amount as well.

With the passing of legislation beginning with the 2007 tax year, there is an exception to the comparability rule. Employers may contribute more to the HSAs of non-highly compensated employees. The IRS uses the same definition of highly compensated employees for HSAs that it uses for other retirement accounts.

Notice Requirement

The notice requirement mandates that employers give employees notice that each eligible employee who, by the last day of February, establishes an HSA and notifies the employer that they have established an HSA, will receive a comparable contribution to the HSA for the prior year. Employers will meet the notice requirement if by January 15 of the following calendar year, they provide written notice to all affected employees.

Contribution Requirement

Employers meet the contribution requirement for these employees, if by April 15 or an IRS-specified deadline, they contribute comparable amounts plus reasonable interest to the employees' HSAs for the prior year.

Cafeteria Plans

The comparability rules do not apply to contributions made through a cafeteria plan. Comparable participating employees in a cafeteria plan:

- Are covered by your HDHP and are eligible to establish an HSA
- Have the same category of coverage (either self-only or family coverage)
- Have the same category of employment (part-time, full-time, or former)

Excise Tax

If an employer made contributions to employees' HSAs that were not comparable, they must pay an excise tax of 35% of the amount contributed.

Employment Taxes

Amounts employers contribute to their employees' HSAs are not generally subject to employment taxes. Employers must report the contributions in box 12 on Form W-2 for each employee, including amounts the employee contributed through a cafeteria plan.

Employer contributions are deductible by the employer as contributions to a health plan.

Required Reporting

There should be no surprises for the HSA owner. He or she should receive periodic statements on how much is in the HSA, how much it has earned in interest or investment returns, fees or administrative expenses (i.e. maintenance, check replacement), and expenses paid out of the HSA.

ERISA Requirements for Private Employer Plans

Two government agencies share most of the federal regulation of private employer benefit plans: The US Department of Labor and the IRS.

ERISA is the federal law that established legal guidelines for private pension plan administration and investment practices. ERISA generally preempts state laws as they apply to private-sector employee benefit plans. For instance, state laws cannot be enforced against an employee benefit plan, even if the state law sets higher standards of benefits than available in the plan.

The Department of Labor enforces participants' benefit rights under ERISA, and the IRS makes sure employers meet the tax code rules that allow them to sponsor and deduct the costs of benefit plans.

HSAs pose new challenges to define and implement a health savings vehicle in an employment setting.

Unless another ERISA exemption applies (i.e. the plan is sponsored by a governmental or church entity), an HDHP offered by an employer is considered an ERISA plan. It is then subject to all the fiduciary, reporting, and disclosure rules imposed on employee benefit plans under federal law. Employers are required to distribute summary plan descriptions, file Form 5500, and meet fiduciary obligations on investments particular to ERISA.

On the other hand, according to the Department of Labor (DOL Field Assistance Bulletin 2004-1), HSAs are not considered ERISA-covered employee benefit plans, as long as the employer's involvement is limited. Essentially, DOL created a safe harbor for HSA plans, meaning as long as these plans meet certain criteria, they are safe from classification as an employee benefit plan. Instead, an HSA is considered by DOL to be a personal health care savings vehicle, rather than group insurance.

This safe harbor exemption from ERISA for HSAs exists even if the employer makes contributions to the HSA, with the following caveats:

- The employer cannot limit the ability of eligible employees to move their funds to another HSA beyond the restrictions provided in the Internal Revenue Code (IRC)
- The employer may not impose conditions on utilization of HSA funds beyond restrictions permitted by the IRC
- The employer cannot make or influence investment decisions with respect to funds contributed to the HSA
- The employer cannot represent the HSA as an employee welfare benefit plan established or maintained by the employer
- The employer may not receive any payment or compensation in connection with the HSA

If an HSA meets these requirements, and therefore is not considered an ERISA plan, it is subject to state law.

Non-ERISA HSAs

An HSA that is not an ERISA plan—either because the employer made that choice or because the account holder did not obtain it through an employer—lacks a key protection other ERISA savings plans have.

Funds the account holder accumulates in an employer-sponsored pension plan are shielded from creditors in the event that the account holder declares personal bankruptcy. Because an HSA is not an ERISA plan, creditors can attach balances in the account to a bankruptcy.

ERISA and Governmental Employer Plans

Federal, state, and local government employers are not subject to ERISA.

The Office of Personnel Management administers federal employee benefit laws. State and local government employees should look to the agencies charged with administering their benefit plans.

States and localities may vary widely on issues of reporting, comparability, eligibility, fiduciary obligations, and record keeping.

CHAPTER 11

Federal and State HSA Laws and Health Care Reform

The Federal HSA Law

Section 1201 of the Medicare Prescription Drug Improvement and Modernization Act of 2003 was signed by President Bush on December 8, 2003, and became Public Law No: 108-173. This provision adds Section 223 to the IRC to permit eligible individuals to establish HSAs for taxable years beginning after December 2003.

On March 23, 2010, President Obama signed the Patient Protection and Affordable Care Act (PPACA). While PPACA addresses a lot more than HSAs, some of PPACA's new requirements for insurance coverage impact how HSAs are used.

State Laws Affecting HSAs

An HSA Is a Trust

A trust is a fiduciary relationship where a bank, corporation, or other entity acting as a trustee holds legal title with a legal obligation to keep and use the trust for the benefit of the equitable owner.

A trustee is a party given legal responsibility to hold property in the best interest of or for the benefit of another entity or person. The trustee is responsible for managing and investing funds. A custodian, on the other hand, is the person or institution in charge of property in terms of maintenance of an account, but with no investment or management responsibilities.

An HSA is a trust because it is owned by the account holder, accumulates funds year-to-year, and is governed by specific uses and rules. As a trust, an HSA is subject to both state and federal law.

An HSA trustee must be a bank, insurance company, or a non-bank trustee (an entity that meets specific IRS requirements).

The trustee must deal with the trust property honestly, put the beneficiary's interest above its own, and closely follow the terms of the trust. Though it may have discretion over investments and day-to-day management, these functions are still governed by the trust agreement. The benefit for which the trustee holds and administers an HSA is for paying qualified medical expenses.

States Define Official Establishment of a Trust

Many state trust laws maintain that an HSA is established or "opened" once funds are deposited in the account.

States may have different rules regarding the establishment of trusts. For example, Utah passed a 2009 law that amended its trust law to allow greater flexibility when determining when an HSA is established. Utah allows the establishment of the HSA to coincide with the date the account holder enrolled in a federally qualified HDHP, provided that the account is opened and funded no later than the filing deadline, without extensions, of the account owner's federal tax return.

State Requirements for HDHPs and Preventive Care

State insurance laws often require health plans to provide certain health care benefits without regard to the deductible, or on terms no less favorable than other care provided by the health plan. For an HDHP to offer preventive care, the IRS defined (and continues to define under PPACA) standards for preventive care—what the plan can pay for without jeopardizing the plan's tax status—rather than adopting the criteria for preventive care applied under state law.

Federal Law Overlap with State Law

A plan that meets federal law may not meet state requirements. In a state where insurance laws conflict with the federal law governing HSAs, you may not be able to enroll in an HSA unless it is combined with an employer's self-insured HDHP. Self-insured plans are governed by ERISA and do not have to comply with state benefit laws.

Exemptions from State Mandates

State legislatures can decide how to best deal with HSAs. Some have enacted exemptions from state mandates for plans that meet federal criteria for HSA-qualified HDHPs.

As a rule of thumb, if your health plan or broker offers an HSA-qualified plan in your state, it is likely legal for you to purchase the plan and contribute to the account.

Different Tax Treatments

It is important to recognize that while an HSA is a pretax savings account under federal income tax laws, it may not qualify for tax breaks under state or local income tax laws, or under the state component of the tax that finances unemployment benefits. State tax law and state estate law may also affect how HSAs are treated.

HSAs and the States*

HSA Policy	States	Total
States that conform to federal IRC for HSA purposes as of December 2004	AZ, CO, CT, DE, GA, HI, ID, IL, IN, IA, KS, LA, MD, MI, MO, MT, NE, NM, NY, NC, ND, OH, OK, OR, RI, SC, UT, VT VA, WV	30
States that changed laws in 2005 to conform to federal IRC for HSAs	AR, FL, GA, IN, IA, KY, MA, MN, MS, NV, NJ, OK, PA	13
States that in 2006 changed laws for HSAs	MA, OH, UT	3
States that changed laws in 2011 to provide state tax exemption for HSAs	WI	1
States that don't provide state tax exemption for HSAs	AL, CA, NJ	3
States that don't have a state income tax	AK, FL, NH, SD, TN, TX, WA, WY	8
States with HSAs for high-risk pool plans	AL, AR, CO, ID, KY, LA, MD, MN, MO, NE, SD, WY	12
States with HSAs for state employees	AR, FL, KS, OK, SC, SD, UT, WA, IN	9

*Table adapted from data compiled by the National Conference of State Legislatures. For more detailed information, see www.ncsl.org/IssuesResearch/Health/HSAsHealthSavingsAccountsandtheStates/tabid/14462/Default.aspx.

How Federal Health Care Reform Affects HSAs

When PPACA was signed into law in 2010, many HSA enthusiasts were concerned that the new law would undermine the success of HSAs. While PPACA is a very complex law with a number of moving parts, many of the outstanding issues have been addressed with regulations, that in most cases appear to work well with and are even quite friendly to HSAs.

A number of these PPACA provisions, including waving pre-existing condition exclusions, removing lifetime and annual coverage maximums, providing first-dollar coverage for preventative care, and changes in purchasing over-the-counter (OTC) medications are discussed below, along with their impact on HSAs and other health care accounts. These provisions of the law are discussed in order of the year in which they became effective.

2010

Pre-Existing Condition Exclusions for Children Eliminated (Effective Sept. 23, 2010)

Health insurance companies cannot exclude children from coverage based on pre-existing conditions. Applies to all employer plans and new plans in the individual market. Will apply to all plans in 2014.

If you are using your HSA to pay for medical care for an excluded child, you now have coverage. Contact your health plan for more information.

Lifetime Benefit Limits Eliminated (Effective Sept. 23, 2010)

Previously, if you exceeded your plan's lifetime benefit limit for a medical condition, you used your HSA to make up the difference.

PPACA prohibits lifetime limits on benefits for expensive catastrophic illnesses, such as cancer. You will no longer have to use your HSA to make up the difference. This provision affects all existing insurance plans.

Annual Limits for Care Will Be Tightly Regulated

The Department of Health and Human Services (HHS) regulates health plans' use of annual limits. Beginning January 1, 2014, health plans will have no annual or lifetime limits on essential health benefits.

If you have been using your HSA to pay for treatments that exceeded your plan's annual limits, you may now be able to have the plan pick up the cost. Contact your health plan for more information.

Health Plans Must Pay 100% for Preventive Services, Regardless If You Have Met Your Deductible

PPACA mandates that all new group health plans and those in the individual market provide first-dollar coverage for preventive services (first-dollar coverage means 100% coverage without the patient sharing the cost through a co-pay or deductible). This no longer applies to grandfathered groups.

Previous legislation allowed HSA-qualified health plans to offer first-dollar coverage for preventive care without disqualifying them for use with an HSA.

For more information regarding preventative care within PPACA, visit http://www.healthcare.gov/center/regulations/prevention/recommendations.html.

Group Health plans (Including Grandfathered Plans) That Provide Dependent Coverage for Children Must Continue to Make That Coverage Available Until Age 26 (Effective Sept. 23, 2010)

PPACA's mandate for insurance carriers to extend coverage to adult children up to age 26 creates an opportunity for parents to make a tax-free gift to their children in the form of an HSA.

However, there are pitfalls to avoid. There may be a gap in coverage for your adult child because of your health plan's enrollment window for dependents.

PPACA does not say the coverage has to be continuous or immediate.

You may have to purchase COBRA coverage for your child while waiting for the new plan year to start. If you do purchase COBRA, ensure that it is HDHP coverage, so that in the event that your adult child no longer qualifies as a dependent on your tax return, you can open an HSA for the child and fund it up to the full IRS limit. Such a contribution will not be deductible on your own tax return, but it will be tax-free for your child.

Be sure to contact your health plan or insurance broker and a tax adviser to discuss your situation.

- Dependent does not mean the same thing for IRS deductions as it does for insurance plans.
  - Not all IRS-qualified dependents can be covered under your family health plan
  - Not all medical expenses can be deducted on a tax return, and you may need to pay those costs from an HSA

  If your adult child is covered under your HDHP but is not considered a dependent when you file your taxes, he/she can open an HSA and contribute up to the full IRS limit for a family, depending on the kind of HDHP coverage.

The following table provides examples. Discuss your unique situation and needs with your health plan and tax adviser, as the rules can change:

Adult Child's Situation	You Can Deduct This Person's Medical Expenses on Your Tax Return	You Can Use Your HSA for This Person's Qualified Medical Expenses	This Person Can Be Covered by Your Health Plan
My child is 25, married, has his own job, and lives out of state—but does not have access to health insurance	No	No But he can open his own HSA and make the full yearly contribution for a family—$6,550 in 2014, depending on the HDHP plan design.	Yes
My child is 25, married, and has his own job—but does have access to his own health insurance	No	No	No
My child is 27, disabled, and living under my roof. I provide all his support.	Yes	Yes	Probably not, because the child is over age 26

Example: Your child turns 24 in October, so eligibility for an HSA starts on the first day of the following month. That makes two months of eligibility for the tax year (November and December).

Adult Child's Situation	You Can Deduct This Person's Medical Expenses on Your Tax Return	You Can Use Your HSA for This Person's Qualified Medical Expenses	This Person Can Be Covered by Your Health Plan
My child is 23, is going to school, and living in my home with her baby. I'm fully supporting her and my grandchild.	Yes, for both your child and her baby. If you continue to support your child when she turns 24, only her baby will continue to be your dependent.	Yes, for both your child and her baby. When your child turns 24, if she and her baby are still being supported by you in your home, you can only use your HSA funds for her baby's qualified medical expenses. However, after she turns 24, you can help your adult child set up her own HSA now that she's no longer your dependent but is still covered by your qualifying health plan. You can even fund her HSA up to the full family yearly amount of $6,550 for 2014.	Your child only—and only until she turns 26. Most plans won't let you add a grandchild to your family coverage. You can cover the baby's qualified medical expenses out of your HSA. If your daughter has her own HSA, she can't use it for her baby because, in this example, the baby is claimed as your dependent.

Example: Your child turns 24 in October, so eligibility for an HSA starts on the first day of the following month. That makes two months of eligibility for the tax year (November and December).

2011

Over-the-Counter Medications Are No Longer Qualified Medical Expenses for HSAs, FSAs, and HRAs

There are exceptions: Insulin and over-the-counter medicines prescribed by a provider as treatment for a specific medical condition still qualify for use with HSAs. Keep your receipts and copies of your prescriptions for use at tax time.

The Penalty Increases from 10% to 20% for Using HSA Funds for Non-Qualified Medical Expenses

After you turn 65, this penalty disappears. However, you will still have to pay income tax on any health care account money spent on non-qualified medical expenses.

All Health Plans Must Spend a Higher Percentage of Premium Dollars on Actual Medical Care Than on Administrative Costs

In 2011, health plans must report on the share of premium dollars spent on medical care. They will have to provide rebates to consumers if guidelines set by PPACA are not met.

This may affect some individuals' eligibility to participate in an HSA-qualified health plan.

New Voluntary Options for Long-Term Care Insurance Are Being Provided

PPACA created long-term care insurance programs to be financed by voluntary payroll deductions as a way to provide benefits to adults who become disabled.

You will be able to participate in this insurance program without losing your HSA eligibility. You may also be able to pay for the premiums from your HSA.

2012

No changes or additions to PPACA affected HSA provisions during 2012.

2013

The Threshold for Claiming Itemized Deductions for Medical Expenses Increased from 7.5% to 10%

If you did not have an HSA or other health care account, you could use itemized deductions to reduce the taxes on money you spent for medical expenses. Previously, your medical expenses had to add up to at least 7.5% of your adjusted gross income before you itemized them as deductions. Beginning last year in 2013, that threshold increased to 10%.

Contributions to FSA's Reduced to $2,500

Effective January 1, 2013, the IRS limited the annual contribution limit of $2,500 for health care FSAs.

2014 to 2017

Health Insurance Exchanges in Each State Provide Insurance to Individuals and Small Groups

Most states will set up a network of health insurance exchanges. These exchanges enable people to comparison shop for standardized health packages. Often times, HSA-qualified health plans will be the least expensive plans on these exchanges. The health care reform law will facilitate enrollment and administer tax credits, so that people of all incomes can obtain affordable coverage.

In 2014, Most Individuals Are Required to Obtain an Acceptable Level of Health Insurance Coverage or Pay a Penalty

The penalty for not having coverage will be $95 in 2014, $325 in 2015, $695 or up to 2.5% of income in 2016, up to a cap of the national average bronze plan premium. Families will pay half the amount for children, up to a cap of $2,250 per family. After 2016, dollar amounts will be indexed for inflation.

If affordable coverage is not available to an individual, they will not be penalized.

All non-grandfathered coverage that is purchased by individuals from insurance companies or through exchanges, or that is offered by small employers to their employees, must meet minimum standards in order to be deemed "essential health benefits (EHBs)." EHBs include coverage for 10 general areas of health services, including:

- Ambulatory patient services
- Emergency services
- Hospitalization
- Maternity and newborn care
- Mental health and substance abuse disorder services
- Prescription drugs
- Rehabilitative and habilitative services and devices
- Laboratory Services
- Preventive and wellness services and Chronic disease management
- Pediatric services, including oral and vision care

Additionally, EHBs will have cost-sharing limits for deductibles ($2,000 single/$4,000 family beginning in 2014) and in-network, out-of-pocket maximums ($6,250 single/$12,500 family for 2014). EHBs must also meet 60% actuarial value (AV) requirements — meaning that the plan must pay for at least 60% of the cost of care that would be covered by a plan that had no out-of-pocket cost sharing requirement.

Federal regulations have recently confirmed that employers' contributions to HSAs will positively affect the AV calculation by counting toward the 60% requirement. By definition, EHBs can be HSA-qualified and still meet the minimum PPACA standards. Many employers are better understanding that HSA-based health plans can meet the PPACA EHB requirements but still be cost effective for them and their employees and help their employees avoid taxes by saving through their HSAs.

Insurers Will No Longer Be Able to Exclude Coverage for Treatments Based on Pre-Existing Health Conditions; Also Prohibited From Charging Higher Rates Due to Health Status, Gender, and Other Factors

Starting in 2014, requirements will apply to all health plans. All grandfathering or exceptions will be eliminated. Premiums will vary only on age (no more than 3:1), geography, family size, and tobacco use.

It is likely that health plans will phase out family rates and charge separate premiums for each dependent. Higher-deductible plans coupled with HSAs will become more important to keep premium costs down.

Annual Limits on the Amount of Coverage an Individual Receives Eliminated

Elimination of annual limits started with some plans in 2010. In 2014, it will apply to all major medical health plans (excluding gap or mini-med plans) without exception. This eliminates the need to pay for supplemental coverage from an HSA or other health care account.

Insurance Companies Will Not Be Able to Drop an Individual from Coverage for Routine Care if the Individual is Enrolled in a Clinical Trial

In 2014, PPACA prohibits insurers from dropping coverage because an individual chooses to participate in a clinical trial, in addition to denying coverage for routine care that they would be covered otherwise. This applies to all clinical trials that treat cancer and other life-threatening diseases.

Until in effect, your health care account is an important safety net for you. If you have to pay for coverage out-of-pocket while in a clinical trial, you at least reduce some of the costs by paying with tax-free dollars.

2018

An Excise Tax of 40% (Cadillac Tax) Applies to Excess Premiums for High-Cost Health Plans

A 40% excise tax will be charged to employers for annual health care spending above $10,200 for individuals or $27,500 for families. The Cadillac Tax health care spending calculation is expected to include the following:

- All employer & employee insurance premium costs, including administrative fees
- All employer & employee contributions to FSAs, HSAs, and HRAs
- Any tax-deductible, supplementary coverage purchased by employer or employee

Costs for stand-alone dental and vision plans are not expected to be included in the Cadillac Tax calculation. The Cadillac Tax thresholds are expected to increase by an inflation adjustment each year, and adjustments will also be made to increase the thresholds for employers with higher-risk occupations or an older workforce. While these thresholds may seem high, medical costs continue to increase rapidly and PPACA adds even more costs to premiums. Some estimates suggest that at current trends, as many as 60% of employers will be subject to some Cadillac Tax by 2018 for exceeding the threshold.

While HSA and other health account contributions will be included in the Cadillac Tax calculations, HSA plans are generally lower cost and can help employers avoid the Cadillac Tax penalties. As employers begin to increase deductibles and other cost sharing in an effort to avoid the Cadillac Tax that will come into play in 2018, HSA account holders are wise to save as much money in their HSAs today to prepare for their future health care costs. HSAs provide the best tax-favored vehicle for Americans to save tax free money for health care.

APPENDIX A

Glossary of Health Insurance Terms

Above-the-line deduction. A deduction that can be taken from gross income before arriving at adjusted gross income (AGI). Examples include IRA contributions, HSA contributions, half of the self-employment tax, the self-employed health insurance deduction, and alimony. The term is derived from a solid bold line on Form 1040 and 1040A above the line for adjusted gross income. A taxpayer can take deductions above the line and still choose whether to claim the standard deduction or itemize deductions.

Annual limit. A dollar limit on the claims and insurer will pay over the course of a plan year. The Patient Protection and Affordable Care Act (PPACA) prohibits annual limits for essential benefits for plan years beginning after Sept. 23, 2010.

Authorization. A health insurance plan's permission to proceed with a medical or surgical procedure.

Balance billing. A bill the participant receives for the portion of an out-of-network provider's bill that the insurance plan doesn't cover.

When a participant receives services from a health care provider that doesn't participate in the insurer's network, the health care provider isn't obligated to accept the insurer's payment as payment in full and can bill the participant for the unpaid amount.

Cafeteria plan. An employee benefit plan that allows employees to choose benefits from among a number of different options, including pensions, FSAs, health insurance, other insurance, and paid time off.

Calendar year. January 1 to December 31 of the same year. The calendar year may be different than the plan year; the latter may be any 12-month period established by an employer or insurer for managing the plan and accounting for benefit payments.

Certificate of Coverage. Written evidence of prior health coverage; required under HIPAA; and provided by the insurer once coverage ends.

An enrollee may need to provide this certificate to be exempt from limitations on coverage for pre-existing conditions. (In most situations, PPACA has eliminated the need for this certificate by prohibiting denial of coverage for pre-existing conditions).

Chronic condition. A condition that lasts indefinitely, or recurs frequently, and can be treated but not cured.

COBRA. Acronym for the Consolidated Omnibus Budget Reconciliation Act of 1985 that provides for the temporary continuation of group health plan coverage after a qualifying event to certain employees, retirees, and family members who are qualified beneficiaries.

An HSA can be used to pay COBRA premiums.

Coinsurance. The percentage of an insurance claim for which the patient is responsible to pay.

Conversion coverage. Coverage under an individual insurance policy when group health plan benefits are lost.

Under federal COBRA rules, employers that offer an individual conversion option to active employees must make that option available to COBRA-qualified beneficiaries as well.

Contribution (for HSA). Deposit to the health savings account (HSA).

Co-payments. Fixed-dollar payments the patient makes for a doctor visit or prescription. For example, many HMOs and PPOs impose a co-payment (sometimes referred to as a co-pay) for an in-network doctor's visit.

Covered services. The medically necessary treatments a plan pays for, at least in part.

Custodian. An entity responsible for the maintenance or administration of an account but that has no investment or management responsibilities.

Deductible. The amount of covered expenses that an individual pays for out-of-pocket before payments are made by the health plan.

Dependent. For a health plan: a dependent that a health insurance company covers under an individual's health plan; not the same as a tax dependent.

In most cases, the health insurance company and state law decide who is a qualified dependent under the health plan. One exception is the federal mandate under PPACA that adult children up to age 26 be covered by a parent's family plan if the child doesn't have access to health coverage from his or her own employer. This coverage is not taxable to the parent. However, the child can only receive distributions from the parent's HSA if the child also qualifies as a tax dependent on the parent's return. If the adult child is covered under a parent's family HDHP, but doesn't qualify as a tax dependent, the child can open his or her own HSA.

For tax purposes: a person who can be claimed as a dependent on your federal tax return. This isn't the same as a dependent on your health plan. Only your spouse and people you can claim as dependents on your tax return can receive distributions from your HSA, whether or not they're covered by your family HDHP.

Distribution (for HSA). Withdrawal from a health savings account (HSA).

Eligible individual (for HSA). An individual who meets all the IRS criteria for contributing to his or her own HSA.

Emergency. The sudden onset of a condition or an accidental injury requiring immediate medical or surgical care to avoid permanent disability or death.

Employee assistance plan/program. An employee benefit that covers all or part of the cost for employees to receive counseling, referrals, and advice in dealing with stressful life issues.

ERISA (Employee Retirement Income Security Act). A federal law that governs private-sector employee benefits plans.

Excess contribution (for HSA). An HSA contribution that's higher than allowed by law.

Exchange. A government-regulated marketplace of insurance plans with different tiers, or levels of coverage, offered to individuals without health care or to small companies; also referred to as health exchange.

PPACA creates new American Health Benefit Exchanges in each state to assist individuals and small businesses with comparing and purchasing qualified health insurance coverage.

Exclusions. Medical services or conditions for which a particular health care plan or policy won't pay.

First-dollar coverage. Benefits that pay the entire covered or eligible amount without requiring a deductible.

Flexible spending account (FSA). An arrangement that allows employees to set aside pretax earnings to pay for benefits or expenses not paid by their insurance or benefit plans. May be free-standing or part of a cafeteria plan. All unspent funds are forfeited back to the employer at the end of the year.

Formulary. The list of drugs covered fully or in part by a health plan.

Full contribution rule. Also last-month rule. See last-month rule and testing period.

Gatekeeper. The doctor, usually a primary care doctor, pediatrician, or internist, responsible for overseeing and coordinating all aspects of a patient's care.

In an HMO, the gatekeeper must preauthorize all referrals, except emergencies.

Grace period (for FSA). The period when the account holder can continue to incur expenses and submit reimbursements after the end of the plan year. After the end of the grace period, any unused balances for the previous plan year are forfeited back to the employer.

Grandfathered plan. A health plan that an individual was enrolled in prior to the passage of PPACA on March 23, 2010.

Grandfathered plans are exempt from many of the immediate changes required by PPACA. New employees may be added to group plans that are grandfathered, and new family members may be added to all grandfathered plans.

Health care reform law. See Patient Protection and Affordable Care Act (PPACA).

Health Insurance Portability and Accountability Act (HIPAA). A federal law that limits the exclusion of pre-existing conditions, permits special enrollment when certain life or work events occur, prohibits discrimination against employees and dependents based on health status, and guarantees availability and renewability of health coverage to certain employees and individuals. It also establishes strict standards for using and sharing private health information (PHI).

Health reimbursement arrangement (HRA). (Sometimes called health reimbursement account.) An employer-owned and funded account from which the employee is reimbursed for qualified medical expenses, such as co-payments, deductibles, vision care, prescriptions, long-term care, medical insurance, and most dental expenses. Reimbursements aren't taxed to the employee, and are deductible by the employer.

High-deductible health plan (HDHP). A type of health insurance plan that, compared to traditional health insurance plans, requires higher initial out-of-pocket spending, although premiums may be lower.

HIPAA. See Health Insurance Portability and Accountability Act (HIPAA).

HMO (health maintenance organization). A corporate entity (for-profit or not-for-profit) that provides or arranges for coverage of certain health services for a fixed, prepaid premium.

Home health care. Skilled nursing and related care supplied to a patient at home.

Hospice care. Care given to terminally ill patients, generally those with six months or less to live and that emphasizes meeting emotional needs and coping with pain. Care may be given in the patient's home or at a facility.

Hospital outpatient department. A facility or area where a range of non-urgent medical care is provided under the supervision of a physician.

Indemnity plan. A plan that pays health insurance benefits in the form of cash payments rather than services.

Individual coverage requirements and penalties. Requirement for most individuals to obtain acceptable health insurance coverage or pay a penalty. There will be no penalty if affordable coverage is not available to an individual.

Individual retirement account (IRA). An account that allows individuals to save for retirement on a tax-deferred basis. The amount that is tax deductible varies according to an individual's pension coverage, income tax filing status, and adjusted gross income.

In-network provider. A health care provider (such as a hospital or doctor) contracted to be part of the network for a managed care organization (such as an HMO or PPO).

The provider agrees to the managed care organization's rules and fee schedules in order to be part of the network and agrees not to balance bill patients for amounts beyond the agreed upon fee.

Last-month rule. IRS rule that allows a participant who enrolls in a qualifying HDHP mid-year to contribute the entire yearly maximum contribution for his or her age and coverage level if the participant is HSA-eligible with an HDHP on the first day of the last month of the tax year (December 1 for most tax payers). Also referred to as the full contribution rule.

The participant must remain eligible for the entire testing period to avoid incurring taxes and penalties. See testing period.

Life event. A change in a participant's personal situation that results in the gain or loss of eligibility for an HSA, a health plan, or a spouse's or dependent's employer's plan.

If a participant experiences a qualified life event, he/she may be eligible to make changes to his/her benefit coverage. Some common life events include, but aren't limited to:

- Marriage or beginning of a domestic partnership
- Divorce or termination of a domestic partnership
- Birth or adoption of a child
- Death of a spouse/domestic partner or child
- Spouse's loss of coverage
- Child's loss of eligibility
- Change in employment status
- Loss of qualified HDHP coverage

Lifetime limit. The limit many health insurance plans place on the claims that the insurer will pay over the course of an individual's life.

PPACA prohibited lifetime limits on benefits beginning Sept. 23, 2010.

Limited benefits plan. A type of health plan that provides coverage for only certain specified health care services or treatments or provides coverage for health care services or treatments for a certain amount during a specified period.

Managed care plan. A health plan that limits costs by limiting the reimbursement levels paid to providers and by monitoring health care utilization by participants or both.

Mandated benefit. A requirement in state or federal law that all health insurance policies provide coverage for a specific health care service.

Matching contributions. Employer contributions paid to the employee's account (HSA, FSA) only if the employee also contributes a minimum specified amount.

Medicare. A federal government health insurance program for people 65 and older, the disabled, and people with end-stage renal disease who require dialysis or a transplant; part of the Social Security system.

- **Medicare Part A.** Pays for inpatient hospital stays, care in a skilled nursing facility, hospice care, and some home health care.

- **Medicare Part B.** Helps pay for doctors' services, outpatient hospital care, durable medical equipment, and some medical services not covered by Part A.

- **Medicare Part C (Medicare Advantage Plans).** A combination of Part A and Part B. The main difference in Part C is that it's provided through private insurance companies approved by Medicare.

- **Medicare Part D.** A stand-alone prescription drug coverage insurance.

Medicare Part D "donut hole." The gap between the maximum spending amount Medicare Part D will cover and the minimum spending amount to qualify for catastrophic prescription drug coverage.

The beneficiary is responsible for 100% of all costs between these two amounts.

Medicare supplement (Medigap) insurance. Private insurance that supplements Medicare and Medicare Advantage Plans. It reimburses out-of-pocket costs not covered by Medicare and that are the beneficiary's share of health care costs.

A participant can't have an HSA if he/she also has Medigap insurance.

Medical loss ratio. The percentage of health insurance premiums spent by the insurance company on actual health care services rather than administrative costs.

The PPACA requires that large group plans spend 85% of premiums on clinical services and other activities for the quality of care for enrollees. Small group and individual market plans must devote 80% of premiums to these purposes.

Medically necessary treatments. Treatments appropriate for the diagnosis, care, or treatment of a certain injury or condition. Check the plan's definition; whether or not a given service is covered may depend on where and by whom it's delivered.

Mistaken distribution (for HSA). Mistaken withdrawal from a health savings account (HSA), such as a non-qualified medical expense or an overpayment to a health care provider. A participant can avoid paying income tax and a 20% penalty on the amount by returning the money to the HSA administrator for redeposit into the HSA.

Multistate plan. A plan, created by PPACA and overseen by the U.S. Office of Personnel Management (OPM), that is scheduled to be available in every state through health care exchanges beginning in 2014.

Network plan. A plan that generally provides more favorable benefits for services provided by its network of providers than for services provided outside the network.

Nondiscriminatory contributions. Employer contributions are considered nondiscriminatory if the employer makes comparable contributions on behalf of all eligible employees with comparable coverage during the same period. Contributions are considered comparable if either the same dollar amount or the same percentage of the deductible under the HDHP.

Open enrollment. A period of time during which employees may change health plans without incurring costs or penalties.

Out-of-network provider. A health care provider (such as a hospital or doctor) that isn't contracted to be part of a managed care organization's network (such as an HMO or PPO).

Depending on the managed care organization's rules, an individual may not be covered at all or may be required to pay a higher portion of the total costs when he/she seeks care from an out-of-network provider. A health plan may disallow applying out-of-network provider costs to the deductible.

Out-of-pocket limit. A maximum limit on the out-of-pocket expenses a participant pays during the plan year.

Amounts a participant pays for deductibles, co-payments, or coinsurance are included in out-of-pocket expenses and kept as a running total. Insurance premiums aren't counted toward out-of-pocket limits.

Once a participant reaches the plan's limit for the year, remaining eligible expenses are covered at 100% regardless of the plan's usual co-payment or coinsurance arrangements. Some plans refer to this limit as the stop-loss limit or out-of-pocket maximum.

Patient Protection and Affordable Care Act (PPACA). Legislation (Public Law 111-148) signed by President Obama on March 23, 2010. Commonly referred to as the health care reform law.

Permitted coverage. Coverage an individual may maintain, in addition to an HDHP, without losing eligibility for an HSA, even though the coverage may provide first-dollar coverage for certain medical expenses.

PHI. Private health information that is strictly protected by law.

Plan administrator. The person or firm designated by a health plan or employer to handle day-to-day details of record keeping, claims handling, and report filing.

Plan participant or beneficiary. An employee or dependent of that employee who is participating in, receiving benefits from, or eligible to receive benefits from an employee benefit plan.

Plan year. The calendar year (January 1 to December 31), or another 12-month period the employer or insurer chooses for managing a health plan and keeping track of deductibles and other limits.

Point of service (POS). A managed care plan that allows patients to see doctors not included in the plan, but for an increased fee; usually found as part of an HMO.

Portable account. An account that can be carried from job to job and from group plans to individual coverage.

Pre-existing condition exclusion. A period of time when an individual receives no benefits under a health benefit plan for an illness or medical condition for which the individual received medical advice, diagnosis, care, or treatment within a specified period of time prior to the date of enrollment in the health benefit plan.

PPACA prohibits pre-existing condition exclusions for all plans beginning January 2014.

PPO (preferred provider organization). An arrangement between doctors and other medical service providers and an insurer to offer services at a discounted rate in exchange for the insurer sending patients to their doctors or facilities. Usually includes some utilization review.

Premium. The periodic payment required to keep an insurance policy in force.

Preventive benefits. Covered services intended to prevent or identify a medical condition while more easily treatable.

PPACA requires insurers to provide coverage for preventive benefits without charging deductibles, co-payments, or coinsurance.

Primary payer. The health care plan that pays its share of covered expenses first when a consumer has access to two different health plans, while the secondary payer pays some or all of the amount left over—even if that amount is less than the secondary plan otherwise pays.

This applies to Medicare when the participant is still covered under an employer plan.

Prohibited transaction. The sale, exchange, or lease of property, borrowing or lending money, furnishing goods, services, or facilities, transferring to, used by, or for the benefit of the beneficiary of any assets contained in the account. Pledging account assets—as security for a loan, for example—constitutes a prohibited transaction.

Provider. Whoever provides health care under a health plan, including doctors, therapists, nurse-practitioners, and anyone else who provides medical services.

Provider discount. A reduced rate a doctor, hospital, or other health care professional or facility agrees to accept when they enroll in a health plan's network.

Prudent layperson standard. Under this standard, emergency care is covered in a health care plan if the decision to go to the ER was one that an average person with average medical knowledge would make at the time.

Qualified health plan. A health insurance policy sold through an exchange.

PPACA requires exchanges to certify that qualified health plans meet minimum standards outlined in the law.

Qualified HSA distribution. A distribution from a health flexible spending account (FSA) or health reimbursement arrangement (HRA) contributed by your employer directly to your HSA. This is a one-time distribution from any of these accounts treated as a rollover contribution to the HSA and subject to the testing period rules.

Qualified medical expense. An expense paid by the account beneficiary or owner, his or her spouse, or dependents, for medical care as defined in section 213(d) of the Internal Revenue Code; generally the same expense that individual taxpayers can deduct on federal income tax returns.

Certain types of health insurance premiums are considered a qualified medical expense for purposes of HSAs.

Referral. A recommendation of a medical professional. In HMOs and other managed care plans, a referral is usually necessary to see any practitioner or specialist other than a gatekeeper physician, for the service to be covered.

Release. Permission for specified medical information to be released to a specific person or entity.

Repricing. The adjustment of health care providers' "sticker price" to reflect discounts the providers may have negotiated with a health plan.

Rescission. The process of voiding a health plan from its inception usually based on the grounds of material misrepresentation or omission on the application for insurance coverage that would have resulted in a different decision by the health insurer with respect to issuing coverage.

PPACA prohibits rescissions except in cases of fraud or intentional misrepresentation of a relevant fact.

Rollover contribution. Transfer of an account balance from one financial institution to another or from one type of account to another.

Safe harbor. When an activity is deemed to meet certain authorized criteria, it will be safe and considered in compliance with law or regulation.

Screening services. Medical tests designed to detect treatable diseases or conditions.

Section 401(k) plan. A defined contribution retirement plan that allows participants to have a portion of their compensation (otherwise payable in cash) contributed pretax to a retirement account on their behalf. The plan is named after the section of the Internal Revenue Code that establishes the rules for the plan.

Self-insured plan. A plan under which the employer pays for medical claims as they arise rather than contracting for coverage from an insurer.

Stop-loss limit. See out-of-pocket limit.

Testing period. The length of time an individual must remain in a qualified HDHP to avoid taxes and penalties if he/she makes the maximum yearly contribution to an HSA under the last-month rule.

If the individual enrolled in a qualifying HDHP mid-year, but contributed the full yearly maximum contribution to the HSA under the last-month rule, he/she must remain an eligible individual during the testing period. For the last-month rule, the testing period begins with the last month of the tax year and ends on the last day of the 12th month following that month. For example, December 1, 2010, through December 31, 2011. See last-month rule.

Transition rule. A gradual adaptation to a law in order to ease the impact of a change on affected taxpayers.

Trend. Medical cost inflation; for example, the yearly increase in the cost of premiums.

Trust. Legal instrument allowing one party (the trustee) to control property for the benefit of another.

Trustee. An entity or individual that directs the investment of the funds in a trust account and has management responsibilities.

Umbrella deductible. A stated maximum amount of expenses a family could incur before receiving benefits.

Usual, customary and reasonable charge (UCR). The cost associated with a health care service that's consistent with the going rate for identical or similar services within a particular geographic area.

Reimbursement for out-of-network providers is often set at a percentage of the usual, customary and reasonable charge, which may differ from what the provider actually charges for a service.

Waiting period. A period of time that an individual must wait, either after becoming employed or submitting an application for a health insurance plan, before coverage becomes effective and claims may be paid.

Premiums aren't collected during this period, and HSA contributions can't begin until the first day of the month after the waiting period ends and HDHP coverage begins.

APPENDIX B

IRS Forms

See www.irs.gov for full details.

- Form W-2 (includes a section for HSA reporting): www.irs.gov/pub/irs-pdf/fw2.pdf
- Form 1040/1040EZ: www.irs.gov/pub/irs-pdf/f1040.pdf

US Individual Income Tax Return

- Form 1099-SA: www.irs.gov/pub/irs-pdf/ f1099sa.pdf

Distributions from an HSA, Archer MSA, or Medicare Advantage MSA

- Form 5329: www.irs.gov/pub/irs-pdf/f5329.pdf

Additional Taxes on Qualified Plans (Including IRAs) and Other Tax-Favored Accounts

- Form 5498-SA: www.irs.gov/pub/irs-pdf/f5498sa.pdf

HSA, Archer MSA, or Medicare Advantage MSA Information

- Form 5305b: www.irs.gov/pub/irs-pdf/f5305b.pdf

Health Savings Trust Account

- Form 5305c: www.irs.gov/pub/irs-pdf/f5305c.pdf

Updates

See www.hsaguidebook.com for recent updates.

APPENDIX C

Qualified Medical Expenses

The IRS provides yearly updates on the medical and dental expenses that are and are not tax-deductible, and therefore payable from an HSA. See www.irs.gov for the most current version of *Publication 502—Eligible Medical and Dental Expenses*.

Following is a list of items that can be include in figuring the medical expense deduction. Items are listed in alphabetical order and, if listed, the amount paid by a participant can be included as a medical expense.

Legal abortion.

Acupuncture.

Alcoholism. Inpatient treatment at a therapeutic center for alcohol addiction, including meals and lodging provided by the center during treatment; amounts paid for transportation to and from Alcoholics Anonymous meetings if attendance is pursuant to medical advice that membership in Alcoholics Anonymous is necessary for the treatment of patient's alcoholism.

Ambulance services.

Artificial limb.

Artificial teeth.

Autoette. See wheelchair.

Bandages.

Breast reconstruction surgery. Following a mastectomy for cancer or other breast disease.

Birth control pills.

Braille books and magazines. For use by a visually-impaired person that is more than the cost of regular printed editions.

Capital expenses. Special equipment installed in a home and other home improvements if the main purpose is medical care for yourself, your spouse, or your dependent.

The cost of permanent improvements that increase the value of a property may be partly included as a medical expense. The cost of the improvement is reduced by the increase in the value of the property. The difference is a medical expense. If the value of the property isn't increased by the improvement, the entire cost is included as a medical expense.

Certain improvements made to accommodate a home for a disabled person don't usually increase the value of the home, and the cost can be included in full as medical expenses. These improvements include, but aren't limited to, the following:

- Constructing entrance or exit ramps.
- Widening doorways at entrances or exits.
- Widening or otherwise modifying hallways and interior doorways.
- Installing railings, support bars, or other modifications to bathrooms.
- Lowering or modifying kitchen cabinets and equipment.
- Moving or modifying electrical outlets and fixtures.
- Installing porch lifts and other forms of lifts (elevators generally add value to the house).
- Modifying fire alarms, smoke detectors, and other warning systems.
- Modifying stairways.
- Adding handrails or grab bars anywhere (whether or not in bathrooms).
- Modifying hardware on doors.
- Modifying areas in front of entrance and exit doorways.
- Grading the ground to provide access to the residence.

Only reasonable costs to accommodate a home for a disabled person are considered medical care. Additional costs for general repair or aesthetic reasons aren't medical expenses.

Example

Making Capital Improvements on a Home

Stephen and Leslie are taking care of an elderly parent who has had a stroke. All the bedrooms and bathrooms in their home are on the second floor. They install an elevator and modify one bathroom to accommodate a wheelchair.

The elevator costs $8,000. An appraisal shows that the elevator increases the value of their home by $4,400.

They subtract the increased value of their home ($4,400) from the cost of the improvement ($8,000). The difference ($3,600) is the amount they can claim as a medical expense.

Construction to widen the doorway of a bathroom and replace the bathtub with a wheelchair-accessible shower costs $5,800. Because the bathroom remodel doesn't increase the value of their home, the owners can claim the entire $5,800 as a medical expense.

Operation and upkeep. Amounts paid for the operation and upkeep of a capital asset, as long as the main reason is for medical care; applies even if none or only part of the original cost of the capital asset qualify as a medical care expense.

Example

Improvements That Increase the Value of a Home

If, in the previous example, the elevator increased the value of the home by $8,000, the owners wouldn't be able to claim any portion of the cost of the elevator as a qualified medical expense.

However, the cost of electricity to operate the elevator and any costs to maintain it are medical expenses as long as the medical reason for the elevator exists.

Improvements to property rented by a person with a disability. Amounts paid to buy and install special plumbing fixtures for a person with a disability (mainly for medical reasons) in a rented house are medical expenses.

Example

Improvements Installed by a Disabled Tenant

John has arthritis and a heart condition. He can't climb stairs or get into a bathtub. On his doctor's advice, he installs a bathroom with a shower stall on the first floor of his two-story rented house.

The landlord didn't pay any of the cost of buying and installing the special plumbing and didn't lower the rent. John can include the entire amount he paid as a qualified medical expense.

Car. The cost of special hand controls and other special equipment installed in a car for the use of a person with a disability.

Car, special design. Difference between the cost of a regular car and a car designed to hold a wheelchair.

Cost of (car) operation. See transportation.

Chiropractor.

Christian Science practitioner.

Contact lenses. Needed for medical reasons (such as correcting vision or protecting the eye); cost of equipment and materials required for using contact lenses, such as saline solution and enzyme cleaner. See Eyeglasses and eye surgery.

Cosmetic surgery (reconstructive). If necessary to improve a deformity arising from, or directly related to, a congenital abnormality, a personal injury resulting from an accident or trauma, or a disfiguring disease.

Crutches. Purchase or rental.

Dental treatment. Includes fees paid to dentists for X-rays, fillings, braces, extractions, dentures, etc.

Diagnostic devices. For diagnosing and treating illness and disease, such as diabetic testing equipment and supplies.

Disabled dependent care expenses. Some may qualify as either: medical expenses or work-related expenses for purposes of taking a credit for dependent care.

This can be applied either way as long as you don't use the same expenses to claim both a credit and a medical expense deduction.

Drug addiction. Inpatient treatment at a drug treatment center, including meals and lodging.

Drugs. See medicines.

Eyeglasses. Needed for medical reasons; can also include fees paid for eye examinations.

Eye surgery. To treat illnesses, injuries, and defective vision (laser eye surgery or radial keratotomy).

Fertility enhancement. Procedures such as in vitro fertilization (including temporary storage of eggs or sperm); surgery, including an operation to reverse prior surgery that prevented fertility.

Founder's fee. See lifetime care—advance payments.

Guide dog or other service animal. To be used by a visually-impaired or hearing-impaired person; the cost of a dog or other service animal trained to assist persons with other physical disabilities; amounts paid for the ongoing care of service animals.

Health institute. Only if prescribed by a physician, and the physician issues a statement that the treatment is necessary to alleviate a physical or mental defect or illness of the individual receiving the treatment.

Health maintenance organization (HMO). Premiums paid for yourself, your spouse, or a dependent to receive medical care from a health maintenance organization. See insurance premiums.

Hearing aids. Also batteries to operate hearing aid.

Home care. See nursing services.

Home improvements. See capital expenses.

Hospital services. Cost of inpatient care at a hospital or similar institution if the principal reason for being there is to receive medical care; includes amounts paid for meals and lodging. Also see lodging.

Insurance premiums. HSA funds can be used to pay for insurance premiums under the following circumstances:

- You're collecting federal or state unemployment benefits.
- You have COBRA continuation coverage through a former employer.
- You have a qualified long-term care insurance contract (subject to additional limitations).

If you have a policy that provides more than one kind of payment, you can include the premiums for the medical care part of the policy if the charge for the medical part is reasonable. The cost of the medical part must be separately stated in the insurance contract or given to you in a separate statement.

Note: If advance payments of the health coverage tax credit are made on an individual's behalf to an insurance company, don't include any advance payments made when figuring the amount the individual may deduct for insurance premiums. Also, if this individual is claiming the health coverage tax credit, the individual can subtract the amount shown on line 4 of Form 8885 (reduced by any advance payments shown on line 6) from the total insurance premiums paid.

- **Medicare Part A premiums.** If covered under Social Security (or if a government employee who paid Medicare tax), an individual is enrolled in Medicare A. The payroll tax paid for Medicare A isn't a medical expense.

  If the individual isn't covered by Social Security (or wasn't a government employee who paid Medicare tax), he/she can voluntarily enroll in Medicare A. In this situation the premiums the individual pays for Medicare A can be included as a medical expense on his/her tax return.

- **Medicare Part B premiums.** Medicare B is a supplemental medical insurance plan. Premiums paid for Medicare B are a medical expense.

  If an individual applied for Medicare B at 65 or after he/she became disabled, he/she can deduct the monthly premiums paid.

  If you were over 65 or disabled when you first enrolled, check the information you received from the Social Security Administration to find out your premium.

- **Medicare Part C (Medicare Advantage) premiums.**

- **Medicare Part D premiums.**

- **Prepaid insurance premiums.** Premiums paid before 65 for insurance for medical care for an individual, a spouse, or dependents after an individual reaches 65 are medical care expenses in the year paid if:

  - Payable in equal yearly installments or more often, and

  - Payable for at least 10 years, or until the individual reaches age 65 (but not for less than five years).

Laboratory fees. If part of medical care.

Lead-based paint removal. The cost of removing lead-based paints from surfaces in the home to prevent a child who has or had lead poisoning from eating the paint.

The surfaces must be in poor repair (peeling or cracking) or within the child's reach. The cost of repainting the scraped area isn't a medical expense.

If, instead of removing the paint, the area is covered with wallboard or paneling, treat these items as capital expenses. See capital expenses. The cost of painting the wallboard can't be included as a medical expense.

Learning disability. See special education.

Legal fees. To authorize treatment for mental illness.

Lifetime care—advance payments. Part of a life-care fee or founder's fee paid monthly or as a lump sum under an agreement with a retirement home.

The part of the payment included is the amount properly allocable to medical care. The agreement must require that an individual pay a specific fee as a condition for the home's promise to provide lifetime care that includes medical care.

An individual can use a statement from the retirement home to prove the amount properly allocable to medical care. The statement must be based either on the home's prior experience or on information from a comparable home.

- **Dependents with disabilities.** Advance payments to a private institution for lifetime care, treatment, and training a physically or mentally impaired child upon the caregiver's death or when the caregiver becomes unable to provide care.

  The payments must be a condition for the institution's future acceptance of the child and must not be refundable.

- **Payments for future medical care.** Generally, an individual can't include in medical expenses current payments for medical care (including medical insurance) to be provided substantially beyond the end of the year. This rule doesn't apply in situations where the future care is purchased in connection with obtaining lifetime care of the type described above (see dependents with disabilities).

Lodging. Cost of meals and lodging at a hospital or similar institution if a principal reason for being there is to receive medical care. See nursing home.

An individual may be able to include in medical expenses the cost of lodging not provided in a hospital or similar institution. The individual can include the cost of such lodging while away from home if all of the following requirements are met.

- The lodging is primarily for and essential to medical care.
- The medical care is provided by a doctor in a licensed hospital or in a medical care facility related to, or the equivalent of, a licensed hospital.
- The lodging isn't lavish or extravagant under the circumstances.
- There is no significant element of personal pleasure, recreation, or vacation in the travel away from home.

The amount included in medical expenses for lodging can't be more than $50 for each night for each person. The individual can include lodging for a person traveling with the person receiving the medical care. For example, if a parent is traveling with a sick child, up to $100 per night can be included as a medical expense for lodging. Meals aren't included.

Don't include the cost of lodging while away from home for medical treatment if that treatment isn't received from a doctor in a licensed hospital or in a medical care facility related to, or the equivalent of, a licensed hospital or if that lodging isn't primarily for or essential to the medical care received.

Long-term care. Amounts paid for qualified long-term care services and premiums paid for qualified long-term care insurance contracts.

Long-term qualified care services. Necessary diagnostic, preventive, therapeutic, curing, treating, mitigating, rehabilitative services, and maintenance and personal care services (defined below) that are:

- Required by a chronically ill individual.
- Provided as the result of a plan of care prescribed by a licensed health care practitioner.
- **Chronically ill individual.** An individual is chronically ill if, within the previous 12 months, a licensed health care practitioner has certified that the individual meets either of the following descriptions.
  - He or she is unable to perform at least two activities of daily living without substantial assistance from another individual for at least 90 days, due to a loss of functional capacity. Activities of daily living are eating, toileting, transferring, bathing, dressing, and continence.
  - He or she requires substantial supervision to be protected from threats to health and safety due to severe cognitive impairment.
- **Maintenance and personal care services.** Care that has as its primary purpose providing a chronically ill individual with needed assistance with his/her disabilities (including protection from threats to health and safety due to severe cognitive impairment).

Long-term qualified care insurance contracts. An insurance contract that provides only coverage of qualified long-term care services.

The contract must:

- Be guaranteed renewable.
- Not provide for a cash surrender value or other money that can be paid, assigned, pledged, or borrowed.
- Provide that refunds, other than refunds on the death of the insured or complete surrender or cancellation of the contract, and dividends under the contract must be used only to reduce future premiums or increase future benefits.

- Generally not pay or reimburse expenses incurred for services or items that would be reimbursed under Medicare, except where Medicare is a secondary payer, or the contract makes per diem or other periodic payments without regard to expenses.

- **Qualified long-term care premiums.** Qualified long-term care premiums, up to the amounts shown below, can be included as medical expenses on Schedule A (Form 1040):

  - Age 40 or under: $330
  - Age 41 to 50: $620
  - Age 51 to 60: $1,230
  - Age 61 to 70: $3,290
  - Age 71 or over: $4,110

- **Unreimbursed expenses for qualified long-term care services.** The limit on premiums is for each person.

Meals. The cost of meals at a hospital or similar institution if a principal reason for being there is to get medical care. The cost of meals that aren't part of inpatient care are ineligible.

Medical conferences. Amounts paid for admission and transportation to a medical conference if the medical conference concerns the chronic illness of an individual, a spouse, or a dependent.

The costs of the medical conference must be primarily for and necessary to the medical care of an individual, a spouse, or a dependent. The majority of the time spent at the conference must be spent attending sessions on medical information.

The cost of meals and lodging while attending the conference isn't deductible as a medical expense.

Medical information plan. Amounts paid to a plan that keeps medical information in a computer data bank and retrieves and furnishes the information on request to an attending physician.

Medical services. Amounts paid for legal or medical services provided by:

- Physicians
- Surgeons
- Specialists
- Other medical practitioners

Medicare Part A: Covers hospital insurance that pays for inpatient hospital stays, care in a skilled nursing facility, hospice care, and some home health care.

Medicare Part B: A medical insurance that helps pay for doctors' services, outpatient hospital care, durable medical equipment, and some medical services that aren't covered by Part A.

Medicines. Medications prescribed by a provider to treat a specific medical condition.

Beginning January 1, 2011, over-the-counter medications (except insulin and medications prescribed by a provider) are only eligible for reimbursement from an HSA or other health care account.

Mentally challenged, special homes for. Costs of keeping a mentally challenged person in a special home, not the home of a relative, on the recommendation of a psychiatrist to help the person adjust from life in a mental hospital to community living.

Nursing home. Costs of medical care in a nursing home, home for the aged, or similar institution, for an individual, a spouse, or a dependent.

This includes the cost of meals and lodging in the home if a principal reason is to get medical care.

If the reason for being in the home is personal, the cost of meals and lodging is ineligible.

Nursing services. Wages and other amounts paid for nursing services.

Services need not be performed by a nurse as long as the services are of a kind generally performed by a nurse. This includes services connected with caring for a patient's condition, such as giving medication or changing dressings, as well as bathing and grooming the patient. Services can be provided at home or a care facility.

Generally, only the amount spent for nursing services is a medical expense. If the attendant also provides personal and household services, amounts paid to the attendant must be divided between the time spent performing household and personal services and the time spent for nursing services. However, certain maintenance or personal care services provided for qualified long-term care can be included as medical expenses. Additionally, certain expenses for household services or for the care of a qualifying individual incurred to allow you to work may qualify for the child and dependent care credit. See *IRS Publication 503—Child and Dependent Care Expenses.*

Part of the amount paid for that attendant's meals is also eligible. Divide the food expense among the household members to find the cost of the attendant's food. Then divide that cost in the same manner as in the preceding paragraph. If additional amounts were paid for household upkeep because of the attendant, these amounts can be included. This includes extra rent or utilities paid because of a move to a larger apartment to provide space for the attendant.

- **Employment taxes.** Social Security tax, FUTA, Medicare tax, and state employment taxes paid for a nurse, attendant, or other person who provides medical care.

  If the attendant also provides personal and household services, the amount of employment taxes paid for medical services as explained under nursing services is eligible. For information on employment tax responsibilities of household employers, see *IRS Publication 926—Household Employer's Tax Guide.*

Operations. Amounts paid for legal operations that aren't for unnecessary/ unprescribed cosmetic surgery.

Optometrist. See eyeglasses.

Organ donors. See transplants.

Osteopath.

Oxygen. Oxygen equipment to relieve breathing problems caused by a medical condition.

Prosthesis. See artificial limb.

Psychiatric care. Includes the cost of supporting a mentally ill dependent at a specially equipped medical center where the dependent receives medical care. See psychoanalysis and transportation.

Psychoanalysis.

Psychologist. Amounts paid for medical care.

Special education. Fees paid on a doctor's recommendation for a child's tutoring by a teacher who's specially trained and qualified to work with children with learning disabilities caused by mental or physical impairments, including nervous system disorders.

An individual can include as medical expenses the cost (tuition, meals, and lodging) of attending a school that furnishes special education to help a child to overcome learning disabilities. A doctor must recommend that the child attend the school.

Overcoming the learning disabilities must be a principal reason for attending the school, and any ordinary education received must be incidental to the special education provided. Special education includes:

- Teaching Braille to a visually impaired person.
- Teaching lip reading to a hearing impaired person.
- Giving remedial language training to correct a condition caused by a birth defect.

An individual can't include in medical expenses the cost of sending a problem child to a school where the course of study and the disciplinary methods have a beneficial effect on the child's attitude if the availability of medical care in the school isn't a principal reason for sending the student there.

Sterilization. Legally performed operation to make a person unable to have children.

Stop-smoking programs. Note that amounts paid for drugs that don't require a prescription, such as nicotine gum or patches, designed to help stop smoking, are ineligible.

Surgery. See operations.

Telephone. Cost of special telephone equipment that lets a hearing-impaired person communicate over a regular telephone; also the cost of repairing the equipment.

Television. Equipment that displays the audio part of television programs as subtitles for hearing-impaired persons; may be the cost of an adapter that attaches to a regular set or part of the cost of a specially equipped television that exceeds the cost of the same model regular television set.

Therapy. Received as medical treatment.

- **Patterning exercises.** For a mentally retarded child; must consist mainly of coordinated physical manipulation of the child's arms and legs to imitate crawling and other normal movements.

Transplants. Medical care received because an individual is a donor or possible donor of a kidney or other organ; and medical care of a donor in connection with the donating of an organ to another individual, including transportation.

- Transportation primarily for, and essential to, medical care, including: bus, taxi, train, or plane fares or ambulance services.
- Transportation expenses of a parent who must go with a child who needs medical care.
- Transportation expenses of a nurse or other person who can give injections, medications, or other treatment required by a patient who is traveling to get medical care and can't travel alone.
- Transportation expenses for regular visits to see a mentally ill dependent, if these visits are recommended as a part of treatment.

Transportation. You can include in medical expenses amounts paid for transportation primarily for, and essential to, medical care.

You can include:

- Bus, taxi, train, or plane fares or ambulance service
- Transportation expenses of a parent who must go with a child who needs medical care
- Transportation expenses of a nurse or other person who can give injections, medications, or other treatment required by a patient who is traveling to get medical care and is unable to travel alone
- Transportation expenses for regular visits to see a mentally ill dependent, if these visits are recommended as a part of treatment
- **Car expenses.** Out-of-pocket expenses, such as the cost of gas and oil, when a car is used for medical reasons are eligible. Depreciation, insurance, general repair, and maintenance expenses are not.

  In lieu of actual expenses, a standard mileage rate for use of a car for medical reasons is eligible. To find the current mileage rate for medical treatment, go to www.irs.gov.

  Parking fees and tolls are eligible whether actual expenses or the standard mileage rate are used.

Trips. Transportation to another city if the trip if primarily for, and essential to, receiving medical services are eligible. See lodging and medical conferences.

Tuition. Under special circumstances, charges for tuition are eligible. See special education. Charges for a health plan included in a lump sum tuition fee if the charges are stated separately or can easily be obtained from the school are eligible.

Vasectomy.

Veterinary fees. Care of guide dogs for the seeing-impaired or hearing-impaired and other service animals specially trained to assist persons with physical disabilities are eligible.

Vision correction surgery. See eye surgery.

Weight-loss program. Amounts paid to lose weight if it is a treatment for a specific disease diagnosed by a physician, such as obesity, hypertension, or heart disease, are eligible, including fees paid for membership in a weight-reduction group and attendance at periodic meetings.

The cost of special food is eligible only if:

- The food doesn't satisfy normal nutritional needs.
- The food alleviates or treats an illness.
- The need for the food is substantiated by a physician.
- The amount included as medical expenses is limited to the amount by which the cost of the special food exceeds the cost of a normal diet.

Wheelchair. Amounts paid to rent, purchase, operate, and maintain an autoette or wheelchair used mainly for the relief of sickness or disability and not just to provide transportation to and from work.

Wig. Cost of a wig purchased on the advice of a physician for the mental health of a patient who's lost all of his or her hair from disease or treatment.

X-ray. For medical reasons.

Ineligible Medical and Dental Expenses

Following is a list of items that can't be used when figuring the medical expense deduction. The items are listed in alphabetical order.

Babysitting, childcare, and nursing services for a normal healthy baby. Amounts paid for the care of children, even if the expenses enable an individual, a spouse, or a dependent to get medical or dental treatment are ineligible. Any expense allowed as a childcare credit can't be treated as an expense paid for medical care.

Controlled substances. Such as marijuana, laetrile, etc., in violation of federal law.

Cosmetic surgery. Including any procedure directed at improving the patient's appearance and doesn't meaningfully promote the proper function of the body or prevent or treat illness or disease, such as face lifts, hair transplants, hair removal (electrolysis), teeth whitening, and liposuction.

Dancing lessons. As well as swimming lessons, etc., even if they're recommended by a doctor, if only for the improvement of general health.

Diaper service. Diapers or diaper services, unless needed to relieve the effects of a particular disease.

Electrolysis or hair removal. See cosmetic surgery.

Employer-sponsored health insurance plan. Any insurance premiums paid by an employer-sponsored health insurance plan unless the premiums are included in box 1 of Form W-2; any other medical and dental expenses paid by the plan unless the amount paid is included in box 1 of Form W-2.

Example

Premiums Paid with Pretax Dollars

You're a federal employee participating in the Federal Employee Health Benefits (FEHB) program.

Your share of the FEHB premium is paid with pretax dollars. Because you're an employee whose insurance premiums are paid with money that's never included in your gross income, you can't deduct the premiums paid with that money.

Funeral expenses. Funeral expenses may be deductible on the decedent's federal estate tax return.

Future medical care. Care to be provided substantially beyond the end of the year is ineligible. This doesn't apply to situations where the future care is purchased in connection with obtaining lifetime care of the type described under long-term care.

Hair transplant. See cosmetic surgery.

Health club dues. Or amounts paid to improve one's general health or to relieve physical or mental discomfort not related to a particular medical condition; the cost of membership in any club organized for business, pleasure, recreation, or other social purpose.

Health coverage tax credit.

Household help. Even if such help is recommended by a doctor, this is a personal expense that isn't deductible. However, certain expenses paid to a person providing nursing-type services may be eligible. For more information, see nursing services. Also, certain maintenance or personal care services provided for qualified long-term care is eligible. For more information, see qualified long-term care services.

Illegal operations and treatments. Or controlled substances whether rendered or prescribed by licensed or unlicensed practitioners.

Insurance premiums. Including:

- Life insurance policies
- Policies providing payment for loss of earnings
- Policies for loss of life, limb, sight, etc.
- Policies that pay a guaranteed amount each week for a stated number of weeks if hospitalized for sickness or injury
- The part of car insurance premiums that provides medical insurance coverage for all persons injured in or by a car because the part of the premium for an individual, a spouse, or a dependent isn't stated separately from the part of the premium for medical care for others
- Medicare Medigap premiums

Legal fees. Management of a guardianship estate, fees for conducting the affairs of the person being treated, or other fees that aren't necessary for medical care.

Maternity clothes.

Medical savings account (MSA). Or medical expenses paid for with a tax-free distribution from an Archer MSA or other funds equal to the amount of the distribution. For more information on Archer MSAs, see *IRS Publication 969—Medical Savings Accounts (MSAs).*

Nutritional supplements. Vitamins, herbal supplements, natural medicines, etc., unless recommended by a medical practitioner as treatment for a specific medical condition diagnosed by a physician.

Over-the-counter medications (except insulin). And biologicals, unless prescribed by a provider to treat a specific medical condition.

Personal-use items. The cost of an item ordinarily used for personal, living, or family purposes, unless used primarily to prevent or alleviate a physical or mental defect or illness.

For example, the cost of a toothbrush and toothpaste is a nondeductible personal expense.

Where an item purchased in a special form primarily to alleviate a physical defect is one that in normal form is ordinarily used for personal, living, or family purposes, the excess of the cost of the special form over the cost of the normal form is a medical expense. See braille books and magazines.

Sick leave (unused sick leave used to pay premiums.) An individual can include in gross income cash payments received at the time of retirement for unused sick leave. An individual can also include in gross income the value of unused sick leave that, at the individual's option, the employer applies to the cost of continuing participation in the employer's health plan after the individual retires. (The cost of continuing participation in the health plan is eligible.)

If an individual participates in a health plan where the employer automatically applies the value of unused sick leave to the cost of continuing participation in the health plan (and the individual doesn't have the option to receive cash), the individual can't include the value of the unused sick leave in gross income. The individual can't include this cost of continuing participation in that health plan as a medical expense.

Swimming lessons. See dancing lessons.

Teeth whitening. See cosmetic surgery.

Transportation expenses. Including:

- Going to and from work, even if the condition requires an unusual means of transportation
- Travel for purely personal reasons to another city for an operation or other medical care
- Travel that is merely for the general improvement of health

Weight-loss program. When for the improvement of appearance, general health, or sense of well-being, including amounts paid to lose weight unless the weight loss is a treatment for a specific disease diagnosed by a physician (such as obesity, hypertension, or heart disease). Includes fees paid for membership in a weight-reduction group and attendance at periodic meetings. Also membership dues for a gym, health club, or spa; the cost of diet food or beverages because the diet food and beverages substitute for what is normally consumed to satisfy nutritional needs; the cost of special food unless all three of the following requirements are met.

- The food doesn't satisfy normal nutritional needs.
- The food alleviates or treats an illness.
- The need for the food is substantiated by a physician.

The eligible amount is limited to the amount by which the cost of the special food exceeds the cost of a normal diet.

INDEX

D

G

H

M

N

O

P

Q

R

S

Y

About the Author

Stephen Neeleman, MD

Stephen Neeleman, MD is the CEO and founder of HealthEquity, Inc. (www.HealthEquity.com), the nation's oldest and largest dedicated health savings trustee based in Draper, UT. Dr. Neeleman founded HealthEquity to help people obtain better health care and save money and to repair the fractured relationship between patients and their physicians.

As a board-certified physician, Dr. Neeleman brings to HealthEquity a passion and firsthand knowledge for the practice of medicine. Prior to his medical training, Dr. Neeleman worked as general manager for Morris Air in Salt Lake City, UT (later acquired by Southwest Airlines). Morris Air combined efficiency, technology, and excellent customer service to succeed in a rocky industry. This innovative business model allowed Morris Air to rise above financially struggling competitors. With HealthEquity, Dr. Neeleman is using this model to help save another struggling industry: American health care.

In addition to his duties as CEO of HealthEquity, Dr. Neeleman is currently a practicing general and trauma surgeon for Intermountain Healthcare at American Fork Hospital and Utah Valley Regional Medical Center in Utah. Dr. Neeleman was appointed by Utah Gov. Gary Herbert to serve as a board member of HIP Utah, Utah's high-risk insurance pool. He also serves on America's Health Insurance Plans' HSA Leadership Council. Dr. Neeleman is a former assistant professor of surgery at the University of Arizona.

Dr. Neeleman completed his undergraduate degree and played football at Utah State University. He attended medical school at the University of Utah and completed his surgical training at the University of Arizona. Dr. Neeleman is married to Christine Lamb Neeleman. Together, they have five children. They love spending time at the family's ranch in Southern Utah.

Key Contributors

Sophie M. Korczyk, PhD

Sophie M. Korczyk, PhD was an economist and consultant with a national consulting practice specializing in research and analysis on employee compensation and benefits with special attention to pensions, health care, and government budget policies in the US and overseas. Some of her clients included AARP, the World Bank, the International Monetary Fund, and a number of not-for-profit associations dealing with employee benefits and insurance issues. She published extensively and was a frequent speaker on compensation, benefits, and insurance issues, as well as on Social Security reform. She testified on these issues before the US Congress and several state legislatures and served as a consultant and expert witness in court cases dealing with employee benefits and compensation. She discussed managed health care issues on The Montel Williams Show, PBS, and a number of radio stations. She was an elected member of the National Academy on Social Insurance, a nonprofit, nonpartisan organization made up of the nation's leading experts on social insurance; a Fellow of the Employee Benefit Research Institute; and a former officer of the Washington, D.C.-based National Economists Club. Sophie passed away in November 2009. Her contributions to help educate people through her writing remain part of her legacy.

Hazel A. Witte, JD

Hazel A. Witte, JD is an attorney and consultant specializing in health science, pension, and benefit issues in the US and overseas. Her clients have included The US Department of Labor, The US Department of Health and Human Services, and the US Small Business Administration, the International Monetary Fund, health care companies, universities, and not-for-profit organizations. Ms. Witte actively contributed to health-related judicial education conducted by the Einstein Institute for Science, Health and the Courts for federal and state courts and international judicial forums Currently she is a consultant for national programs, ASTAR–The Advanced Science and Technology Adjudication Resource Project in Washington, DC, where she is developing training materials on novel evidence and health care cases for courts. Ms. Witte has published numerous books and articles and is a member of the District of Columbia Bar.

Joint Projects

Sophie Korczyk and Hazel Witte have extensive experience as consumer educators and authors, particularly on health issues. They are coauthors of *The Complete Idiot's Guide to Managed Health Care,* (New York: Alpha Books, 1998). Recommended by The Washington Post as "... well worth a day's read-through..." for its consumer-friendly information, the book is included in many consumer health education lists. Their publication *HIV/AIDS and Health Insurance* was featured in the Centers for Disease Control "Business Responds to AIDS" campaign. Their *2000 Executive Compensation Deskbook* (San Diego, CA: Harcourt Brace Professional Publishing, 2000) is a comprehensive source of information on data and analysis dealing with executive compensation. In "Managed Care Plans in Rural Areas" (Washington, DC: National Rural Electric Cooperative Association, 1991), they compiled a series of case studies detailing the challenges and opportunities health plans face in rural communities.

Olivia Neeleman

Editor of the 6th and 7th editions of The Complete HSA Guidebook.

Olivia graduated from Washington State University in December, 2011. She currently works in the Marketing Department at HealthEquity, Inc.